Battered
Hope

CAROL GRAHAM

FIRST EDITION

ISBN: 978-1-939748-06-5

Library of Congress Control Number: 2013936900

Published by
NewBookPublishing.com, a division of Reliance Media, Inc.
515 Cooper Commerce Drive, #140, Apopka, FL 32703
NewBookPublishing.com

Printed in the United States of America

Disclaimer: The views and opinions expressed in this book are solely those of the authors and other contributors. These views and opinions do not necessarily represent those of New Book Publishing and Reliance Media Inc.

To protect the privacy of others, names have been changed.

Reliance
Media

Foreword

This memoir, a therapeutic process in countless respects, evolved over many years. Painful memories were relived in order to share them with you, the reader. It is the story of my life consisting of diverse traumas that seemed to attack me unaware each time. I was never prepared for, but always found the strength to endure, the struggles that were often overwhelming.

I chose to write my memoir in the form of a novel which will hold your interest as the story unfolds. It is a story of strength and tenacity. It is a story of a woman who never gives up hope in the most hopeless of circumstances.

Without the encouragement and push by family and friends, this book would never have been brought to completion.

Much appreciation to my husband who shared the pain I endured through my lifetime. It was challenging for him to read my book as it stirred many emotions and memories he had chosen to bury. He gave me advice and helped me remember details I had forgotten. Even though he had been through many of the conflicts with me, he was amazed at how I drew him into the story and kept him wondering what was going to happen next.

I give huge kudos to my daughter, Rochelle, who would not listen to my excuses for not completing the book. She assisted in a major rewrite and making the content run smoothly. She suggested the cover design and the title. When I would get discouraged, she knew how to address my concerns. Her comments:

As Carol's daughter, I always knew that one day I would be writing an introduction to her story. Her journey through life was far from easy, but through sharing her struggles, she promises to give others the hope and strength to never give up. "Life will go on and it will get better" is one of the many lessons she has taught me. Carol is not just my mom; she is my friend, guide, and shoulder to cry on. Her story and strength have made me the strong and confident woman I am today. For the readers of this novel, my hope is that it will be the friend, guide and shoulder you need to cry on. -- Rochelle

My loyal and dear friend, Sharon, always seemed to know when I was struggling and many times at my lowest point, the phone would ring and it would be Sharon asking, "Are you okay?" She was a constant support for over 20 years.

Like many of us, Carol's life started out with big dreams that were quickly destroyed through many circumstances out of her control. But Carol found a way, even at her lowest points, to share with the hopeless and broken and give them the compassion and empathy they needed to make it through their own struggles. She has shown unbelievable endurance through hopeless situations. -- Sharon

I was fortunate to have an editor, Shelley Harrison Rae, who went above and beyond what most editors would do. She listened to my frustrations and encouraged me through each step. When I wanted to stop writing, she told me I couldn't because she wanted to read the end of the story!

Carol, your book has some mystery to it and is so full of trials and tribulations that it is impossible to imagine going through all of it and coming out the other side. It keeps you reading just to find out how you survive and if there is any bright side to it all...which there is. It offers up hope to anyone suffering what seems like insurmountable hardships. There were times when I thought, "Oh, no! Not again!" When you trusted people another time after being cheated or let down or undercut so many times before. The message and theme to me was 'blind trust and perseverance will eventually pay off.' -- Shelley

Special thanks to my dear friend, Leigh, who always gave me positive input and helped me understand how this memoir would be a source of encouragement for others. Leigh and Garnet gave me their financial support to bring this manuscript to print much sooner than would have been possible without it.

Other than my editor, daughter and sister, no one has read my manuscript. I did not want anyone else to read it until it was completed. Because of the painful circumstances I relate in the story, I did not want to be influenced by my friends' comments or questions until it was finished. Yet, I felt compelled to share it with my close friend, Beatrice, and asked her to critique it chapter by chapter. She wholeheartedly agreed and by the fourth chapter cried many tears not understanding why I had to endure so much pain.

Shortly after the seventh chapter was written, she was killed in a tragic boating accident. The evening before she died, I shared an anxiety with her and her last words to me were "Don't worry about anything; you know God will get you through it!" I miss her terribly.

My sister, Dee, helped me tremendously in preparing my manuscript for print and contributing so much to bring it to the final stage.

Great writing job, sister! You have a knack at making it interesting – must say I wanted to shake you a few times when you kept signing property over to others. If I felt that intense about it even though I already knew a lot about your life, I imagine readers will feel the same and really get involved in the story. -- Dee

I urge each of you to cry with me and rejoice with me as you read my story and realize deeply that each trial only makes you stronger and wiser.

Chapter One

The silence was deafening. The only sounds I heard were coming from inside my head. I could hear the blood rushing through my veins from the palpitations of my heart. My sweater was moving to the uneven rhythm. I had to keep telling myself to remain calm. I must not appear flustered or guilty. I tried taking deep breaths to slow down the pace of my heart which took every ounce of my strength and fortitude. I grabbed my knees with both hands in an effort to stop them from shaking. But that didn't seem to help, and fear prevented me from thinking rationally.

How had this Saturday become so different from any other? Saturdays were reserved for house cleaning. That had been drilled into me since childhood. "Don't make plans because Saturdays are for cleaning." Always were – always would be. Sundays were for relaxing but Saturdays meant cleaning. All these years later, I still kept Saturdays for cleaning.

The day started out just like any other Saturday. No one could have guessed that my life was about to change forever. How could one fleeting moment, one microsecond of a person's life make such a difference? If only that moment could be snatched back from eternity, erased, but that was impossible.

It was one of those days when I felt grateful to be alive. It was bright and sunny and the air was fresh from a light snowfall the night before. I cleaned the house with a fury to have everything in order before going to the airport to pick up my husband, Paul. He had been in England for a week on a speaking tour and I was so excited about seeing him and hearing all about the trip. Our four-year-old son, Jason, was helping with the business of the day getting ready for Daddy's return.

The next thing I knew I was in the police station, alone, and scared. The holding room was like a phone booth with no windows. I was sweltering under a choking fog of body odor and stale cigarette smoke. Nausea swept over me and I had to force myself to take a breath.

"You wait here," a man said gruffly. Then the door was slammed shut and locked. That sound resonated through me and I felt as though my life was ending. It sent shivers up my spine and made me shudder. I could not explain my emotions or why I was so scared because I wasn't even sure what was going on. My mind raced. It was an emotional whiplash between "why" and "what if." What was going to happen? Why were they holding me? What if they found Paul? What would happen to my son? The questions wouldn't stop and I could not think clearly. I felt sick to my stomach completely oblivious to the fact that deep within my belly, new life was growing.

Earlier that day, Jason and I picked Paul up at the airport as planned and headed home. We had lots of plans for that evening and the next few days. Then I was arrested and restrained by rude, pushy, border police. They said they were holding me for questioning but I didn't know why. The only thing I knew I should do was to pray, and I wasn't sure how to pray in such a situation.

A gentle, yet firm, voice inside me was saying, "Admit to nothing. *Only* tell them your name and address. Say nothing else. Be careful, because they will try to trip you up." I did not totally understand this, but the voice got louder and louder until I knew I had to obey. I didn't know what was about to happen, but I knew I had to get through this one moment in order to get back home with my husband and son. If only I could snap my fingers and make this all go away.

We had been home from the airport just long enough to take off our jackets when the doorbell rang. I looked at Paul, only to see him flee through the back door without his jacket or shoes. The bell rang again. I had to answer it. The doorknob was cold and slippery and my hands felt weak. I kept telling myself to get control and appear unruffled.

I opened the door and three plainclothes officers filed in, showing me their badges. One of them deliberately shoved me out of the way. I felt violated and terrified. Another one asked me my name and read me my rights before saying, "You have just brought an illegal alien across the border, and we're going to hold you until you tell us where he is."

Our Doberman stationed herself between Jason and me. She was extremely agitated and showing her teeth. One of the officers pulled out his pistol and held it in position to shoot our pet right in front of my son. Things were spinning out of control. I was scared and getting angry. I couldn't believe what was happening. I felt lightheaded, like I might pass out. The man lowered his gun and began speaking in a loud, condescending tone, asking if I had any weapons in the house.

Jason exclaimed, "You want weapons? I got weapons!" They followed him into his bedroom, all three with pistols drawn, as my innocent unsuspecting four-year-old opened his bottom dresser drawer and exposed all his "weapons." The three towering men looked into the drawer. One had the gall to search through the toys in great anticipation of finding something illegal. My son beamed with pride to have real policemen interested in his plastic revolvers and holster. If I hadn't been so scared, I might have laughed.

In a small, locked room from where I found myself a short time later, I could hear the police on the other side of the closed door. It was reporting an ongoing sniffer dog search through the woods behind my house. After all the years he'd spent hunting with his father, now Paul was the prey. The 40 acres were dense, dark, and swampy. I wondered if Paul had watched me being shoved into the patrol car. He would be frozen out there, in only a short-sleeve shirt. I was so worried because I didn't know what was going to happen. Would I ever see him again? I didn't even get to hug him or kiss him good-bye. I bit my tongue to stop a tear from running down my cheek, trying to appear unflustered.

With no findings to report, the police were getting frustrated. Through the closed door, I heard one say, "Those dogs are useless mutts sometimes."

I smiled to myself, feeling a moment of temporary relief. Finally, someone opened the door to my hellhole and said "Follow me."

I had to concentrate on not tripping as my legs were the consistency of Jell-O. I told myself I must not appear weak. I was led into a dingy office that smacked of Government Issue paint. The entire room lacked color. There was a distinct odor of mold. A quick glance around the room showed nothing personal, not even a plant. The desk was covered in files, and I could not help but wonder if they had information about me in one. I demanded to know what they had done with Jason.

"You better talk and talk fast lady if you want to get home to that kid of yours anytime soon," one of them said.

Even under that threat, I knew I must listen to the gently nagging voice inside my head telling me to "say nothing." The pressure was building and the voice was getting louder. I did have the presence of mind to ask, "Don't I get one phone call at least?"

Reluctantly, one of the officers handed me a phone book. I randomly picked an attorney from the yellow pages and dialed the number, trying to keep my hand steady, so I would not show my nervousness. The lawyer said the exact same thing as my inner voice, adding, "Be careful what you sign." I wondered why he'd mentioned signing something.

The questions were quick and repetitive. "Where is your husband?" "Where did he go?" "Do you realize you have broken the law?" "Why did you bring him here?" "Where has he been?"

The interrogation continued but I stood my ground and did not waver. Amazed at my own courage, I had a strong sense that I must obey my inner voice. After ten or fifteen minutes, another officer entered the room. He looked unkempt in a wrinkled suit. His tie was crooked and didn't match his shirt. I found it odd I should notice something that insignificant but it gave me a little more courage. He bent down and whispered something into another officer's ear. It seemed they were going to let me go.

"Read this release form and sign on the bottom," he told me.

I sensed irritation in his voice and assumed he was upset that they had to release me. I looked the form over. It basically said I was being released for lack of evidence. I was about to sign it when I felt compelled to turn it over. At the bottom of the page, in print almost too small to read was a statement admitting my guilt.

I could not believe that such deception would be used in America. I stood up and threw the paper across the desk. "What kind of a game is this?" I raged. "There is no way I'm signing this form!" My adrenalin was rushing, which gave me the audacity I needed to hold my head up high and walk out of there.

It was only about a mile to my house and walking gave me time to think. My hands were quivering, my stomach ached and I needed to go to the bathroom. I knew that if I could just get home I would be able to think clearly. The tears flowed easily now and I tried to keep them at bay. I had to keep my head clear. I had to figure out what to do. Should I get Jason? They had taken him to a daycare, and I felt he was better off there than seeing me in this state. I didn't know if I should stay at home and wait for the phone to ring or start driving around. Would I be followed? There were no answers – only a lot of questions.

I was still very frightened. I was in a cold sweat and my hands were shaking. I tried to button up my sweater but I was all thumbs. Every time I took a breath, my chest hurt. The cold air was helping to clear my head, but I didn't know of anyone I could call or trust.

I had no idea where Paul was, what had happened to him, or how we ended up in this situation. I later learned that Paul could see our home from his crouched position in the woods and watched closely as a figure in the back bedroom kept motioning him to move forward. He assumed it was me, so he obeyed. However, I didn't do that, and other than the officers looking at Jason's toys, no one was in that back bedroom. So he began his trek through the dense forest with no idea of what he was going to do.

Then he heard the voices. There were several. They were coming closer and his heart momentarily stopped. He held his breath as a German shepherd approached him. He knew it was over. The chances were slim to none that he would ever escape. The hunter had found his prey and would be duly rewarded. Paul's heart was pounding so fast, he was afraid the dog would sense his fear and attack. Oddly, the dog just sniffed Paul and relieved himself on a bush.

Then the strangest thing happened. The dog let out a slight yelp and jumped back, like he was being slapped by something unseen, and quickly ran away. The voices diminished and then they were gone. Paul's relief was overwhelming and he felt weak as his adrenalin slowed down, but the task at hand was to find safety. It was not safe to go back home. Now what? Go where? What was happening on the home front? Then he remembered the figure in the back bedroom motioning him to move onward and so he did.

Nothing in my upbringing had prepared me for what was ahead.

Chapter Two

My parents were born in Europe in a small German village in Poland. They lived only a few miles apart but did not meet until their families had immigrated to Wisconsin. They were married in 1927 and had five children.

In 1944, my oldest sister was diagnosed with rheumatic fever and died within a few months. Her death ripped my parents' hearts out. They could not believe a God of love would take their perfect little girl. My father was a minister and this was not supposed to happen.

The night she died my father became very angry with God. He shook his fist and bellowed, "I will never preach again!" Although he never completely understood, in time, he realized God did not cause her death.

Four years later, I was born. I was nothing at all like the quiet and refined sister who had passed away. My oldest brother had already graduated from high school and was in college. My next brother was ten years older than I was, and my other sister was almost seven years older. I was the late-in-life baby who turned the household upside down. My parents were not nearly as strict with me as they had been with my siblings, and I imagine they thought I was spoiled.

I was a sickly child with an innate teenaged attitude. When I was a baby, my parents said they didn't get a decent night's sleep for many months. Often, my dad would fall asleep while walking me, and I would scream when he stopped. I had him around my little finger, even then. And I had inherited a stubbornness and tenacity that would help me cope later in life.

When I was nine months old, death almost snatched me. If it hadn't been for my parent's prayers, I would have died as I had stopped breathing for several minutes. But, there was a plan for my life and God honored my father's faith.

My mother was very ill with liver disease during my entire childhood, and my memories of her are vague, possibly too painful to recall. What I remember most is watching her struggle with a lot of pain. I would often hear her groan and cry softly even though I tried not to listen. If I didn't hear it, maybe it was not happening. Sometimes I would sneak a peek into her room and would see the tears running down her face.

I knew she did not want me to see her that way and respected her privacy, but it was difficult knowing that there was absolutely nothing I could do to make it all go away. I don't ever remember her having a friend. She was very much alone; and later in life, many years after she was gone, I felt great sympathy for her. She was kind and gentle and spent a great deal of time in prayer – mostly for other people but few people ever got to know her.

We had roast beef or chicken dinners on the Sundays she was able to go to church; but more often than not, she would stay at home in bed, too sick to go out. Dad and I would shop for her clothes and the groceries. He would often take me to Sears Roebuck or Robert Hall and buy me clothes. I loved those times but had wished my mother could be there. My friend told me that I needed to start wearing a bra when I was about ten years old. I did not know what size I was or how to determine my size. So, I assumed I was the smallest size and bought a 28AAA. The first day I wore it to school, I almost passed out. It was so tight that I could not breathe. I quickly realized that I should try a larger size. Those were the type of things I never wanted to disturb my mother with, but wished I could.

My parents' bedroom was quite large. That was a good thing because my twin bed had to be in there as well. My brother and my sister each had their own rooms and my sister refused to share with me. My bed was next to my dad's side of the bed, and I often would ask him to hold my hand until I fell asleep. I think I was afraid that I would be left alone and it frightened me. As much as I wanted to believe my mother was going to get well, I feared she would not get any better. The thought of losing her was more than I could endure.

When I went to school in the morning, my mother was in bed. When I came home for lunch, she was in bed and that's where she spent most evenings. Many times her room was not open to me. She was in too much pain and could not be disturbed. She needed total quiet and darkness.

When the doctor came, I knew what it meant. I would go

out of the room and cry. Her agonized groaning would stop when he gave her a shot so she could sleep, but it hurt me to know I would not see her because she would sleep for days.

Mom was never able to attend any of my school activities including my high school graduation, but the memories I hold dearest are the times I came home from school on my lunch hour to snuggle with her in her bed. We ate frozen, sugar-coated cherries and listened to a soap opera on the radio. Sometimes after school we would snuggle in her bed and eat sunflower seeds and read.

I lived with guilt thinking, "If only I were a better person, she would not suffer so much."

I became very close to my dad and we spent a lot of time together. When he visited members of his parish, he would take me along. I watched him help people with their problems and try, at all costs, to mend a marriage. He dealt with every imaginable predicament that families were faced with in the 1950s.

Perhaps that's what made me a "fixer" always trying to find a solution for everyone's dilemma, and spending sleepless nights trying to figure out answers.

On Saturdays, Dad and I would clean the church. He would sweep the floors and vacuum the carpets. I cleaned the bathrooms and the Sunday school rooms. I hated the job because there were so many things I would rather be doing, but I did get paid one whole dollar above my weekly allowance of 25 cents. I spent hours making plans how to spend all my money helping people. I wanted to send money to my missionary brother in Africa so that he could come home sooner because I missed my nephews. I wanted to save enough to buy my mother a pretty dress. I wished I had enough money to make my mother better.

The church was a small German church in Detroit, Michigan. It seemed like I lived in the church, being the pastor's daughter. I was there for any and every type of service.

I loved growing up in the big city of Detroit. I was in the eleventh grade when my dad retired and we moved to Wisconsin, to a totally different way of life.

My health continued to deteriorate and by the time I was 15, I suffered intolerable headaches. As directed by our family physician, my father took me to a psychiatrist who diagnosed that I was under too much stress. There seemed no relief. My mother was dying, my father depended on me for many things, and I was living under the strict regulations of a minister's daughter.

After our move, I did begin to enjoy a bit of a social life. We attended a large church and I got involved with the youth group. We organized a fundraiser for a mission organization. The winning prize was a trip to New York City to the World's Fair. The person who raised the most money would win first prize. I organized a car wash. I went door-to-door and asked for donations. I called every relative I knew and asked for a donation. No one knew who the winner was and it was going to be announced at a banquet. The boy and the girl who raised the most money would be crowned king and queen and each win a free trip. I was very excited. I knew I had a good chance of winning and that I would not be able to afford the trip if I didn't win. I was surprised and elated when they announced the winners. I had raised the most – even more than my male counterpart.

We travelled by bus with a group to New York City. There were about 25 of us including the chaperones. It was a highlight of my young life. We stayed at the Teen Challenge Center in New York City and spent several days in training to help street people. In the evenings, we went to coffeehouses in Times Square and Greenwich Village to listen and share with hurting kids – kids living on the street, kids who had been abused and kids with serious drug addictions. I knew many of them had to be runaways and was so thankful for my warm bed and pastel colored room back home. It was a side of life I knew existed but had never seen. As a teenager from a small town in Wisconsin, I had never seen anyone strung out on drugs or living on the street. Here it seemed to be normal. Most of the people we saw in Harlem were downright scary. They had torn dirty clothes. Many were lying on the sidewalk. Their eyes were empty but full of pain at the same time. We were constantly being asked for spare change. When we walked past the alleys, we would often see people shooting heroin into their veins. I just couldn't believe my eyes that this actually was going on. It was 1963. It was our goal to bring them to the Teen Challenge Center and help them turn their lives around.

It was our 'job' to talk to these kids and let them know that there is someone who loves them, who does not care what they had done but accepts them unconditionally. Often they would see our sincerity and realize that we only wanted to help them. Many would come with us to the Teen Challenge Center and get food and a warm bed and hear about a God who could change their lives.

The New York World's Fair was another highlight of our trip. I had never been to anything like that in my life. On our way home, we stopped in Philadelphia and Washington D.C. experiencing a piece of American history that made an impression on me. I was glad to be alive, to be living in a free country and to have a warm, safe home. The dark streets of New York seemed so far away but I never forgot what I had seen.

Settling back into my sheltered home life after my summer in New York, I felt deprived of doing anything fun. No dancing. No bowling. No movies. No television. No make-up or nail polish. Even the wearing of slacks was taboo. I dearly loved my parents, but I could not understand all their unfair, imposed boundaries. My minister father only permitted me to date Christian young men. I convinced myself that a non-Christian wouldn't want to date me anyway so, without rebelling, I dated Christian young men. There was such a limited number to choose from and any one I really liked wasn't the least bit interested in me.

My only hope of meeting someone was going along with my father on his regular family visitations. I loved it when we visited the families with young men, but father insisted they remain friends and nothing more.

Everything changed when I met Joe at youth group. He was tall and handsome. I had never seen anyone with such a large smile. His eyes seemed to laugh and dance when he smiled. He seemed to really care about me and allowed me to talk about my concerns and problems. It bothered me a lot that his upbringing had been so different from mine. When I met his family, I was shocked. Their home was very dirty. There were seven kids in the family and his younger sister already had a baby of her own. They smoked in the house and always had alcohol around. I knew in my heart that I should end this now, but Joe seemed so needy and so glad that I was his girlfriend. No one had ever really paid much attention to him. He was rather loud and obnoxious. He did things when we were out that were very embarrassing. He brought attention to himself such as drinking a bottle of ketchup in a restaurant or saying embarrassing things to make the waitress blush. I knew better but still stayed with him. I rationalized that he was a good Christian boy, and I would be able to help him and his family. I had been so desperate to start dating that I accepted his offer to start going out together.

We had fun together. We went on a weekly outing with the church youth group sometimes travelling to a nearby town for a concert or a movie. It didn't take long for him to say that he loved me and I told him I loved him too. Because I had an early curfew, I would bring him home with me and we would sit for hours in the living room and listen to music. I thought this was love – doing things I enjoy with someone else. I got used to his ways and ignored them even though he embarrassed me most of the time we were out with other people.

My parents made it clear that he was not the one for me, but I was strong willed and anxious to be a wife and mother. I was a fixer and had convinced myself that I could fix anything that might go wrong. The wedding plans began, against my parents' wishes. I never saw past my love for Joe and was determined to be married. My sister tried to warn me. My brother tried to warn me. My pastor tried to warn me. But, I was in love and determined to make it work. I lost all my close girlfriends while dating Joe. They saw right through him and wanted no part of our relationship. Years later, I realized I had been in love with romance misinterpreted for true love.

Joe's dark side started showing as he became more and more controlling He demanded that I dress to please him which was quite risqué and it bothered me. He didn't want me to have any friends and would not allow me to go anywhere. I suppose if I had been head-over-heels in love, that is where I would have wanted to be, but he seemed to be getting more peculiar. He would sit for hours and memorize the dictionary. He would make me sit there and listen to him read it out loud. Then, the next day, he would use all these new words to impress people. Most weren't impressed, including me. He made more demands on me than my parents had. Deep down that was one of the reasons I wanted to get married. I had wanted someone to take care of me and allow me to have fun without restrictions. It wasn't happening as I had planned. I wanted romance – I got none. This wasn't enjoyment. I finally realized this was something I could not fix – I had had enough and decided to break it off. Joe became seriously morose. His depression was unbearable and he threatened to kill himself if I left.

"If you leave me, I won't have anything left to live for. You don't want me to end up like the rest of my family. God does not want you to leave me. You have made a commitment to me." He would cry and beg and I relinquished. Maybe now he would change realizing how serious I was about him changing.

I was only 18 but I still couldn't share this with my parents. It was all too disturbing and my mother was so very ill. In that day, women were subservient to men and expected to obey them. The only choice I believed I had was to marry him.

All I ever wanted was a home with a white picket fence and children. I wanted to be the best wife and mother the world had known, no matter what the circumstances. In the 1960s, most girls my age wished for the same. I would make the best of it – I did love him to a degree and I would have children to fill my life. It had to work. Surely, I thought, things would improve.

I had the wedding of my dreams; the romantic day I had planned since I was a little girl. My dress was stunning and I looked like a model bride. Nothing could have been more perfect. It was well organized, carefully planned and absolutely gorgeous. With such an incredible wedding, a wonderful marriage would surely follow. Things had definitely improved. At the time I did not realize it was only because I was so busy with all the preparations. Joe had moved to Minneapolis to attend college so he wasn't around much. We talked on the phone often and it was mostly about the wedding and what our life together would be like. The wedding was in our church hall with about 400 people in attendance. Several guests said it was the most beautiful ceremony they had ever witnessed. Many of my aunts, uncles and cousins came a great distance to attend. I had organized everything myself, attending to every detail and making a wedding just like the magazines had shown.

My mother was getting worse, but I was so busy with the wedding I tried to ignore what was happening to her. Three weeks before the wedding, she cried when she told me she could not find a dress to fit her. She was so small and frail but her stomach had swollen so much that she looked nine months pregnant. I told her she was beautiful, and we found a dress that had a long jacket to hide her large waistline. When I came down the aisle with my father, I handed her a long stemmed rose and kissed her sweet cheek. I realized how difficult it was for her to sit there and how much pain she must be enduring.

We had planned our honeymoon on a small lake about 100 miles from home. We rented a cabin that was quaint and romantic. However, while still on our honeymoon, I wondered if I had made a terrible mistake. I tried suppressing the doubting thoughts, but they overwhelmed me. "Do you honestly think he will change?" I was hoping that making love would make a difference but I did not feel loved, just used. "Is it ever going to be any more than this?" "What have I gotten myself into?" It was too late now. I had taken a vow for life. Marriage was forever.

The cancer that had surged through my mother's body finally took its toll and three months after we married, she died. I was too young to lose my mother. I needed my children to have a grandma. I needed her advice and I needed to feel her arm around me, her ear to listen and her shoulder to cry on. How could I possibly go on without her support?

Heartbroken and ridden with guilt, I convinced myself that I had made my tender mother's life difficult and possibly caused the cancer that ate away at her. I had watched her suffer my entire life, but I still hoped she would always be there for me. Now she was gone and her death left a hole in my life and in my heart.

Years later, my father told me that her last words were to ask him to take care of me. She must have known I would need special treatment. She didn't want to leave this earth with her baby needing her. Dad assured her it was time for her to go, she had suffered so much. She closed her eyes and died. She was gone. She was gone. She was……gone.

Funeral arrangements were underway and Joe was adamant that I not attend under any circumstances. "Your mother influenced too many areas of your life and I am determined to break her influence!" I could not believe what I was hearing. My mother was the kindest, sweetest, gentlest creature on earth. What was he talking about? I realized he needed to be in control of this and every area of my life.

The pain was so intense with the loss of my mother; I ignored his demand and went to the funeral, fully prepared to suffer the consequences. I had no idea what that suffering would mean. I just knew I was going to say goodbye to my mother, and he wasn't going to stop me.

Control was a major source of satisfaction for Joe. He had written up a contract and asked me to sign it. When I read it, I refused and he said he would make me very sorry if I didn't. The contract stated that I agreed I would never bear children. Young and naive, without experience to guide me, I signed it in fear of what he might do if I didn't, hoping to change his mind down the road.

Joe only wore black, from head to toe and wanted me to do the same. His whole world seemed dark and sullen. I was becoming fearful of this young man who was supposed to sweep me off my feet and build a white picket fence for me with children and dogs running in the yard. I would be making cookies and delicious dinners for the man I loved. My dream was quickly fading.

After five years of feigning bliss while hiding the pain inside, I had to tell my father I was planning to leave Joe. I just couldn't bear any more of his emotional and mental abuse. He played mind games, making me believe I was worthless, unattractive and would never amount to anything and manipulating me into doing things I knew were wrong. He wanted to swing with another couple. The idea was so foreign to me and completely repulsive. He was overly possessive and never trusted me. If I was late getting home from work, I would get the third degree. If I called a friend, he wanted to know what we discussed. Every penny I earned had to be accounted for. His control was affecting every area of my life. I was living in fear and didn't know what to do. He had become more obnoxious and embarrassed me terribly, especially in front of my family. He was loud and would say dim-witted things trying to show how important and intelligent he was, and I was mortified to be with him. I was unable to change him – he just got increasingly worse.

There was no doubt that my dad would demand I stay with Joe forever – divorce wasn't even a word in his Christian vocabulary – but I had to be honest with him. My father had remarried a year after my mother had died. He was happy again. He had cared for my mother for so many years, cooking the meals, cleaning the house, running up and down the stairs to her room to bring her water and food and whatever she needed. I was so glad to see him smile and enjoying life. At my request, he and my stepmother travelled 400 miles to visit me. They expected me to announce that I was pregnant.

Instead, I blurted out, "I'm leaving Joe. I can't take it any longer!"

Dad smiled, let out a huge sigh of relief and said "Praise God." He knew. He quoted I Corinthians 7:27-28 which paraphrased says – not to leave your spouse; but if you do, you have not sinned.

This was coming from a minister who was from the old legalistic school. My mouth fell open in disbelief. Dad had changed -- he was beginning to understand God's grace and mercy and recognized that I had made a terrible mistake and God would forgive me just as he had. I was his baby girl whom he had watched suffer all those years but had never indicated he had seen my pain.

The next step would not be so easy. I had to tell Joe. "What do you mean you are leaving me? We took a vow before God and you can't leave me. What have I done to make you want to go? I can change. I will buy clothes with color. Please tell me what you want me to do," Joe begged. He would do anything – anything – all I had to do was tell him what to do.

His reaction gave me a glimmer of hope. Maybe he could change. Maybe this marriage was meant to be, after all. Whatever I asked of him, he complied. But I was growing tired of suggesting changes, even though he was most accommodating. It felt like "too little, too late."

I had grown calloused through the years of abuse and realized he would never change, not really. After several months, I engaged a lawyer and began divorce proceedings. It seemed pretty cut and dried. It would be over soon.

No matter where I went, work, shopping, or church, I had the eerie feeling that someone was watching me, but whom and exactly why was a mystery.

It was a warm, bright spring day. I was walking towards my car on the way home from work and was unaware that I was being followed. Without warning, a leather gloved hand was over my mouth. It had an indiscernible taste and smell. Two more hands grabbed my arms and twisted them behind me. Another gloved hand covered my eyes. I thought I was going to die from fright. I almost passed out in fear and tried to scream and kick but couldn't break free from the hold. I kept wondering how many were holding me. One of them was tying a blindfold over my eyes, and I was pushed into my car. Someone held my mouth open while another poured a sweet drink into it. As I was forced to swallow, I felt at least two pills in my mouth and my effort in trying to spit them out was useless. My mouth was held shut and someone plugged my nose. I was praying and crying and I knew I was about to die. I was feeling faint and then ….. Nothing.

I woke up in my car hours later on a dark street. I was completely disoriented and very scared. In and out of consciousness, I knew there had been more than one man on top of me but had no idea who they were or why this happened. I only had flashes of what had happened, bits and pieces that were all a blur. I couldn't remember where I had been. I was hurting in every way; physically, emotionally, mentally and spiritually. Earlier I thought I was going to die and now I was wishing I had. It hurt to try to move. I didn't know how I was going to get home. I could not think clearly. I tried to cry out for help but when I opened my mouth, nothing came out. My clothes had blood on them and my skin hurt. Even though I was totally unable to help myself, I felt guilty and dirty.

Someone must have seen me struggling. I have little memory of that angel of mercy who came along and helped me get home. I have no idea who was helping me but was so relieved to have those strong arms helping me walk. I was fading in and out and vaguely remember getting home. The next thing I knew I was safe and my saviour had disappeared. I thought I could sleep forever and didn't know if I would ever wake up. I wanted a bath but was afraid I would fall asleep in the tub and drown. I collapsed onto my bed.

I had been violated, I felt sick and very sore. But I went to work the next day and never told anyone what had happened. I was afraid Joe would find out and use it against me in the divorce. Days later, a note came in the mail. I recognized the handwriting on the envelope and knew it could not be good news. It was Joe's handwriting and he was making outrageous demands. He wanted me to send him $2000 and my engagement ring. I was to take full responsibility for all the credit card debt, the mortgage on the house and relinquish ownership of the car. He would let me have the dog and the furnishings. This was unbelievable. I had been the "breadwinner." I had bought everything, and it was all in my name. I had a well-paying job as an office manager of a large commercial construction company.

He had pictures of these monsters raping me. He threatened to distribute them to my pastor father and his eight brothers, all ministers. He said he would send a letter with the pictures showing my father what kind of girl I was. This would destroy my father. I once again found myself under the kind of pressure I had faced at eighteen – marry me or I'll kill myself. Violated and so very much alone, I saw no option except to comply.

I didn't have any close friends left but I had to tell someone. I confided to our pastor; and although he was very compassionate, he used my story to illustrate a sermon. Everyone knew who he was talking about and, again, I felt desecrated on top of my pain. People began to ostracize themselves from me. To make matters worse, Joe had gone ahead and sent the pictures to my father and some of my uncles in spite of my meeting his demands. Everything had always been a game to him. He enjoyed winning. My father never mentioned it to me, but I can only imagine how it must have hurt him.

I could not go on. I was humiliated, scared, tired and lonely. My only way out was to end the pain by ending my life. I didn't have any sleeping pills. I didn't know what to do except to use my car as my weapon and drive into a cement wall.

I had tried. I had failed. No one really cared anyway. I didn't think about how this would make me "look." I didn't stop to consider how this would affect my family. I couldn't fix this and just wanted it to end. Speeding towards a cement barricade-- it would all be over soon. I knew if I went fast enough, I wouldn't suffer. My pain would be over and I would be free!

I knew just the place. I drove far enough out of town where there would be little traffic. As I approached the bridge I picked up speed. I pressed the accelerator to the floor and closed my eyes. I tried not to think about what I was doing. I just wanted the pain to end quickly. At the very last possible second, my car somehow pulled itself out of the way of the wall. It was as if something had taken the steering wheel away from me. Instinctively, I grabbed the wheel to keep the car on the road. Suddenly I realized that I could possibly be hurting someone else, that my car could kill someone else. The car was rocking back and forth as I tried to gain control. I thought for sure it would flip over into oncoming traffic. It was all over in a matter of seconds but seemed like it took forever to stop. I was shaking, crying and could not believe what just happened. What had I been thinking? I suddenly realized how selfish my actions were. I had been having a pity party that got out of control. I started to get angry at Joe and what he was doing to me and saw how he had manipulated me and this was just another one of his tricks to control me.

I knew my faith had once again saved my life. I was not sure why but I was being given a second chance. I saw a glimmer of light, a hope that lasted long enough for me to get home and think things through.

We sold our home when we separated and I moved into an apartment. My apartment was not as nice as the new townhouse Joe and I had purchased. But it was home and Joe had never been there – there were no memories of him there. It was my haven. I was no longer a naive sheltered little girl but had grown into a strong, focused and determined young woman who would never find herself in that vulnerable position again. God had given me the strength to survive and to begin life again.

I don't know why Joe didn't continue to fight me, but I was granted my divorce. I washed my hands of this man and started living life. After telling the attorney my story, I was able to walk away clean and free from Joe and his agenda. At least that is what I thought. I thought it was over. However, I had underestimated his anger and could not have imagined what he was capable of doing.

Chapter Three

I was at a roller-skating party hosted by the youth group in my church when I saw Paul. I instantly liked him. Talking with him I sensed many qualities and appreciated how different he was than Joe. Even at 22, he was self-assured and showed incredible potential in anything he set his mind to do. He was already successful in the business arena. When I heard him speak at our church, I knew he was the one. I just knew it! He was a minister's son and going through a divorce so I knew we would have lots in common. However, Paul didn't seem to want anything to do with me. I was very disappointed but I was a determined, strong, stubborn young woman. I had learned a thing or two about how to be in the right place at the right time. I was a typical female with a mission. It was easy to plan to be in the same places he would be and create situations for me to run into him. So, the chase began until I let him catch me!

When I drove in from work one particular Tuesday, I noticed a new XJ6 Jaguar parked about a block away from my home. It looked just like Paul's car. "Strange," I thought, "why would he be parked on my street?" I walked in to find him sitting in the living room.   Excited, concerned, but very much intrigued as to why he was there, I calmly sat down and let him explain. He shared his marriage woes. He knew what I had gone through and thought I would possibly understand.

He married his high school sweetheart contrary to his better judgement. He actually threw up before walking into the sanctuary, knowing he shouldn't go through with the wedding. But it was too late, or so he thought. To save face and his family's embarrassment, he pulled up his bootstraps and proceeded into the church. Embarrassed and sad, he told me their three-year marriage was never consummated. I watched this tender man share his pain and my heart grew warmly attracted to him, even more than it already had been. I could never imagine him treating anyone like Joe had treated me.

We quickly fell in love – the kind of love you read about and see in the movies. This would last a lifetime. We could jump any hurdle. We were meant to be together. There was no doubt. This was not a rebound relationship for either of us and the more we saw each other, the more we knew the feelings were mutual and genuine.

It was amazing how much our backgrounds were similar. Paul was born as the last child of three in Saskatchewan, Canada. His father was a minister.

When Paul was just a baby, he contracted polio. It crippled one entire side of his body. His right arm was twisted behind his back and his right leg was bent under the thigh of his left leg. Doctors didn't give his parents any hope and said he would never be able to walk or use both hands.

One cold November Sunday morning, Paul's dad went to the

church to start the furnace for the morning service. He knew he served a God who cared and answered prayer, but was frustrated and could not understand why his infant son had to suffer. As he prayed and prepared for the morning service by loading the stove with coal, he had a strong sense that everything was going to be okay. He knew in his heart this was the truth and because of his strong faith, prepared himself for a miracle.

As he walked from the church back to the house, Paul's mother came running out the back door screaming, "Paul is healed! Paul is healed!" There had been a miracle, even quicker than Paul's dad expected.

"I walked into Paul's room to give him his morning bottle. When I went to hand it to him, he reached with BOTH hands for it!" She was almost screaming with delight as tears were running down her cheeks. Paul never had the use of his withered right hand before.

"I knew it would happen but just didn't expect it so soon. There is no denying it is a miracle." She took her husband into the bedroom and there was Paul, holding his bottle with both hands. The withered side of his body had become totally straight. He was completely and totally whole. Dad picked Paul up and held him close thanking God for healing his little boy.

Paul told me about the year he turned twelve. They were closing the family cabin for the winter and had to store their vehicles. There was only one driver for two vehicles. His dad decided to tow the Jeep over to a friend's farm using the family car and a long chain. Paul was told to steer the Jeep.

They stopped to fill up with gas and Paul went into the corner store to buy some candy. He was deciding how much to spend when he heard what seemed like an audible voice that said "Spend it all, you won't be able to spend any for a long while." He spun around to see who had spoken to him but saw no one.

The voice went on, "There is going to be a car accident but you are going to be okay." He was terrified to tell his father. He didn't want to look like a sissy by not wanting to go through with helping him steer the Jeep. His dad demanded his sons to be tough.

So, he got into the Jeep and piled blankets and pillows up next to him in hopes of diving under them in case of an accident. Several miles down the road, his dad turned onto a gravel road where a grader was levelling two ridges of piled up gravel. They had to cross over the ridges in order to pass the grader. Paul was trying to steer over the two-foot high ridges when the Jeep began to sway out of control. The chain snapped as the Jeep rolled. Paul was thrown out the driver's window and into the ditch. The entire weight of the vehicle landed on top of him upside down. The impact was so hard, the Jeep bounced up about ten feet into the air, over the fence, and landed on its wheels in the neighboring field. His dad jumped out of the car and ran back to see if Paul was okay. He was sitting up in the ditch in shock. Several of his teeth were knocked out, but amazingly he had only suffered some scrapes and bruises; no broken bones.

When they looked over the situation, Dad made a strange observation. "Look how large the dent is in the roof of the Jeep where it landed on top of you." His dad was shocked. "That is sure odd, how in the world could this be? It just wasn't logical. There is just no way your body could have made that large of a dent." Many times over the years Paul wondered the same thing, but never had an answer. He was just glad to be alive.

Years later, he knew that God had not only warned him of the accident but had protected him as well. It was the only explanation. An angel must have created that large dent in the Jeep taking the full impact for him.

As a teenager, Paul lived in a town that had a large number of steep hills. One day, he and his buddies were speeding down one of them on their motorcycles and were almost in the intersection when Paul realized he had no brakes.

"Stop the traffic!" he screamed in terror. It was only a matter of seconds but his friends did the best they could by shrieking and swinging their arms to stop traffic. He had two choices: go through the red light or make a right-hand turn. He negotiated the turn but hit an oncoming car at 40 miles per hour.

What happened next defied reality. His buddies stood and watched this unfold as if in slow motion. The bike hit the car head-on. Paul was shot straight up into the air. He was held there by unseen hands as he watched his motorcycle being demolished. He looked down and smiled at his friends who were staring up in disbelief. After the screeching of brakes stopped, Paul was set gently on his feet. Paul walked over to the driver of the car to see if he was all right. Once again, what might have been meant for evil was turned into good. Paul couldn't help but wonder if this was the same guardian angel who protected him before.

After attending college in California, Paul traveled internationally with a Christian musical group. Their talent and message took them into many third world and Communist countries. One Christmas, while in South Africa, he bought some diamonds. Stateside, he sold them for considerably more than he paid and decided this was a business worth pursuing.

Even though he had made this decision, he knew deep down that this was not what he was meant to do. He knew he was to minister and teach. He decided he would do both.

By the time I met him, Paul was making several trips a year to South Africa buying diamonds; and on one of these occasions, asked if I wanted to come along. We could visit my missionary brother. I was so excited. Nobody traveled to Africa in the 1970s. What stories I would have to tell. What an opportunity to see this amazing beautiful country.

We did some fabulous sightseeing. We traveled to Kruger National Park and I will never forget the sound of the lions roaring during the night. It was incredibly scary and sounded like they were right outside our hut where we were sleeping. Actually, sleep was not an option. It was just too terrifying listening to the sounds of the jungle in the absolute blackness of the African night. Returning to Johannesburg, we took the train downtown every day. Paul would conduct his business and I shopped. The shopping was incredible. The European designers and unique boutiques seemed endless and the prices were so much less than I had ever seen anywhere else. I loved every day we spent there. I imagined what it would be like to live in such a beautiful place and those thoughts seemed so romantic.

Because of my brother's missionary status, he was able to take us into areas where white man was not allowed and we saw how the

Native Africans lived. This was quite different than what I had seen in the other areas of South Africa we visited. It was heartbreaking to see those living conditions. Many families lived in homes made from cardboard and rocks. My brother shared how he would often see murders that were never reported. Life seemed to have little value and this made a lasting impact on me.

When we took the train into Johannesburg, we would ride the 'white' train. Here we would sit comfortably and read the newspaper or drink coffee. The 'black' train was parallel to us, so close we could reach out and touch it. That train had pushers who would stand outside the doors when the train stopped and push more people on board. They were packed in so tightly you could see their faces pressed against the windows. It was just too troubling. I came in eye-to-eye contact with one of them and could see the hatred generated towards me. I was fearful and on edge but there was nothing I could do about it. It was best not to look. Even decades later, I can still see their faces and sense their anguish.

It was difficult for my oldest brother in South Africa to accept Paul as my future husband. His views on marriage did not include divorce and even my father could not convince him otherwise. We never really discussed it but rapidly became estranged. When I wrote letters to him, they would remain unanswered. I was cut off and it grieved me deeply. I ached for my brother's love and acceptance. It was odd. Days, sometimes weeks, maybe even months passed without thinking about my brother. Our estrangement worked a bit like grief. I have been told that during times of bereavement time heals all wounds. That is not true. In reality, you are devastated, you mourn, you cry to the point where you think you will never stop – and then you reach a stage where survival instinct takes over. You stop. You simply won't or can't let yourself 'go there' anymore because the pain is too great. You block. You deny. But you never really heal.

It was a difficult decision, but Paul and I felt it would be better if we moved away from old memories and judgemental people. We loved the community we were living in but there were too many painful feelings and wounds. Paul wanted to go back to Canada where he had grown up, and he convinced me that we would have a fresh start. Everything was packed and ready. We planned to drive on ahead to the new frontier and the movers would arrive in a few days.

However, everything was put on hold for a couple weeks because Paul decided to fly to South Africa on a buying trip before making the drive cross-country. It was a good excuse for me to go to my sister's in Wisconsin, knowing it might be a long time until our next visit.

I was watching television with my sister and family one evening when I began to feel ill – feverish, achy and tired. I went to bed thinking I had the flu but awoke at three in the morning in excruciating pain. It felt like my back was on fire. The slightest movements made me scream out but my screams went unheard. I had no strength to raise my voice much above a whisper. I couldn't walk. This was definitely not the flu! What was happening to me? I managed to roll out of bed and land hard on the floor. I attempted to crawl but it was more like inching my way across the floor until I got to the bottom of the stairs. I tried again to make some noise but still did not have the strength to make much of an impact. Finally, my sister woke and found me; white as a ghost, in extreme pain, at the bottom of the stairs.

My sister and her husband managed to carry me into the back seat of their car and get me to the hospital, where I was admitted for observation. I was quarantined and terrified. My thoughts raced – was I being punished for my choices?

It took about three days for them to diagnose the problem as spinal meningitis. The doctor said "One more day and we would have lost you."

All I wanted was for Paul to come rescue me. I knew he would be home soon but it was so difficult to wait.

I had no idea what was happening back in Minneapolis. I was sick and alone and away from home. Then, while still in the hospital, I got a telephone call from Paul's dad. I was glad to hear from him but his voice sounded strained. His words were breathy and his voice shaking. It sounded like he was going to cry when he said, "The police just called me to say Paul's house has been vandalized. There was virtually nothing left."

"Excuse me? What did you say?" I knew that I was on medication and wondered if my thinking was foggy.

"The inspector said it looks like a gang – the damage is so extensive. They must have had a great time, even swinging on the chandeliers. They left holes in the walls, the drapes were spray-painted and the white furniture sprayed black. The food in the freezer is strewn across the house. They even took the time to open canned food and spread it around. A fire was started on the living room carpet. Both of the cars in the garage were smashed." He said he did not want us to see it, because it would make us ill. "Oddly," he said, "The only things in the entire house that weren't damaged were your clothes." I have never been able to understand that. Did they run out of time? Did they miss my boxes? It will remain a mystery.

The new owners were to move in at the end of the month. The house they purchased from us was now just a shell. On top of it all, our insurance had lapsed by a few days. A technicality had been overlooked – to the insurance company's advantage.

The damage to the house alone was $49,000, (which at the time was a lot of money), and that was not including any of our furniture, vehicles or personal belongings. A neighbor had given a description of a man snooping around the house. There was no proof, but I knew it must have been Joe. I knew what he was capable of and it nauseated me.

The doctor said, "Try to relax Carol. You are a very sick young woman. Stress is not good in this situation!" Try to relax? How was I supposed to do that? Did he think he could relax in my situation?

A few hours later, I received another phone call from my father-in-law. I could tell from his voice it was not good news. I listened but became anaesthetized and could not believe I was actually hearing him correctly. Our partner in our diamond business was a friend first and then a partner. We had known him long enough to trust him. Apparently, we should not have.

Dad said, "I know this is going to be very hard for you to believe and it is just as difficult for me as I liked Dave. But, he cleaned out your bank accounts, took the entire inventory you had in the office and the safe and split to Las Vegas." Did he really just say that or was I still feeling the effects of the medication?

The ruthless mongrel took us for more than $100,000 in cash and inventory. We had been honest, fair and trusting and this was our reward. My life was spinning out of control. I had no answers, just lots of questions. I was scared, lonely and very ill.

Another person may have understandably blamed God but I couldn't go there. Of course, I questioned why, but received no answer. God would help us through this nightmare; I just didn't know how!

I wondered if Paul knew what was going on. It was the middle of the night, but I had to call him. I could not wait until the morning. I asked the nurse to help me to a telephone and I dialed the number of the President Hotel in Johannesburg, South Africa.

"Paul Graham's room please." The phone rang several times.

"Hello," he answered with a voice I hardly recognized. "You sound tired, are you okay?" I asked.

He poured his heart out, telling me that his father had called and we had lost everything; our business, our home, even our personal belongings. "I feel so guilty; I should have seen it coming. Why did I trust him? Why did he do this to us? What do we do now? Thank God you called," he said with tears in his voice. "I felt desperate. I failed you and I didn't know what to do. I saw no way out. I climbed up onto the railing of the 19th floor balcony ready to jump when the telephone startled me back to reality. If you hadn't called just now, I would have jumped."

The more I heard, the more I knew I had to be strong in the

situation. I hadn't realized it at the time, but nurses told me later that my entire body was shaking and cold to the touch. There had to be answers somewhere. "We will start over." I assured him. "We'll find a way. We're young and intelligent and driven. This is not the end for us, Paul. This is just a new beginning."

When I got off the phone, one of the nurses was staring at me with a gaping mouth. She helped me back to bed and I fell asleep. The next morning I asked her, "Did my husband call last night?" I had a vague recollection of talking to him.

"But don't you remember you called him. I helped you to the phone myself." Surely she was mistaken.

"What do you mean I called him?" I thought she was kidding me.

She proceeded to tell me the events of the night. I had asked for the phone and dialed an operator. I asked for the President Hotel in Johannesburg and then Paul's room. "Are you sure you don't remember doing that?" I assured her I had absolutely no recollection of that and then she told me what she had overheard. It was obvious to her that I was trying to calm him down and encourage him. She had listened in amazement.

When Paul eventually returned home, he filled me in on the details of my phone call and to this day I have no recollection of that night.

When we got back to Minneapolis and saw the condition of our house, we fell toward each other barely able to stand. We took a quick walk through and realized it was a total loss. Nothing was worth salvaging. The boxes of dishes were smashed. There was glass everywhere. Even my beautiful convertible parked in the garage was a write off. All we could do was borrow money to repair the house for the new owners and move out West as planned. This was not the way we had intended to start our new life together.

After the move, things started looking up. We were married by a Justice of the Peace with two witnesses. This was quite different than the first time around. This time I was marrying for love. We restarted our business, and worked hard to get it going again. It didn't take long to start doing well and we were settling into life on the Pacific Coast.

We were anxious to start a family. Paul wanted children as much as I did and there was so much pain around the 'agreement' I had signed with Joe promising him I would never bear children. We found out that a close friend of the family had a baby and due to circumstances in her life could not keep him. We agreed to adopt him and the day we brought him home from the hospital we were thrilled beyond any joy we had ever experienced. It was easy to forget all the recent past while holding the future in our arms. He was beautiful. We named him Seth, and he was ours.

Paul was making two or three trips a year to South Africa on business and I was content in my life as wife, mother and secretary. Paul asked his best friend, Jim, to watch out for me and help me if there was anything I needed while he was gone. One evening Jim called and asked me to come over to get a duck – he had just gone hunting and knew that we would enjoy it for Paul's homecoming. I went to his house with Seth and we chatted for a couple minutes.

Jim started acting weirdly and told me, "You must know I

have always wanted to be with you. Paul will never need to know. We could have some good times while he is traveling."

I was shocked to hear this coming from Paul's so-called 'friend.' "Why are you staying with that loser anyway?"

He started towards me and he seemed even larger that his six foot plus frame. My mind was racing. I knew I had to get out of there but didn't want to appear too anxious. But, my hesitation and caution got the best of me and before I found my car keys and collected my son, he forced me onto the sofa and tried to get my clothes off. I was pushing at him and screaming. Seth knew there was something wrong and started to cry. All of a sudden my adrenalin kicked in and like a mother bear needing to save her cub, I found the strength to throw the large beast of a man off me, pick up my son and escape. We made it home safely but I was considerably shaken.

I decided never to tell Paul what happened. Jim was his childhood friend and he spoke so highly of him. How could I possibly tell him what he had done to me? I had escaped and would never allow myself to be put into that situation again – it was settled, I would say nothing.

The next day I met Paul at the airport. He got off the plane, walked towards me, and without even saying hello he said, "Jim raped you!" My mouth dropped open and I almost fell over. I had not told a soul. No one else knew – how did he know?

He began to tell me what happened on his flight. It was the middle of the night and he was sleeping on the long trip over the ocean. He was awakened with a deep urgency to pray for me. He had no idea why. He prayed for over forty-five minutes until he felt relieved that I was safe. He also had a strong sense as to what had happened.

I begged him not to say anything to Jim, as I did not want this to hurt their friendship. Jim never knew that I told Paul but their friendship was basically over.

It was the mid-1970s and life was finally getting back on track. We worked together in a beautiful suite of offices in downtown Vancouver, B C. I took our precious little boy with me to work every day and life finally seemed to be what I had always longed for in a marriage.

A year had passed since we adopted Seth and when the phone rang that day I had no reason to suspect anything unusual. Paul answered; and as I watched the expression on his face change rapidly, I did not like what I was observing. He called me over to him to share the receiver.

"I am getting pressure from my parents to raise my son and so I am going to have to get him back. We are prepared to hire an attorney if we need to and you know you will not win." The words had been rehearsed and seemed so easy for her to say. A couple sentences, that's all it was -- a couple sentences that tore our hearts out.

"I'm afraid you don't really have a choice," our lawyer informed us. The law was clear. If we chose to fight it, there would only be more pain and great expense. "I will set it up for you so that you can return the child as soon as possible".

RETURN THE CHILD as soon as possible. I screamed on the inside. I cried on the outside. No, this just can't be happening. We loved Seth. He was ours. Again, the bottom of my world dropped out from under me. I loved him and cared for him. He was part of our family for a whole year. I could not imagine life without him. I was his mommy. How could she do this to us? How could she possibly love him like we did? What about Seth? He would be torn from his parents, his home. Surely he would feel the rejection.

We considered all our options and realized we had no choice – short of running away to a foreign country and hiding. He had to go back. Paul reluctantly dialed her number and made the arrangements to meet us at the Vancouver airport. I methodically packed our son's things; his favorite toys, his clothes, his blankie. Tears dripped on everything as I placed them gently into a small bag. The hole in my heart was getting bigger by the second. I didn't know I could hurt this much. Even the past had not prepared me for the pain of relinquishing my son to someone who had not wanted him! But we had no choice. Return the child. Give him back.

I watched from a distance as Paul handed him to her. It was in slow motion. I watched his hands leave the child as he lifted our son into her arms. He was handing my son to a stranger. I wanted to run and grab him but I was glued to the floor. I felt petrified. I thought I was either going to faint or throw up. My hand fluttered to my mouth for a moment fearing I might scream out. How could I go on? Where would I get the strength? This just could not be happening. It was just a dream and tomorrow I would wake up and everything would be normal again.

I could only imagine how empty Paul felt. He had loved his son deeply. We didn't speak about this much over the years as it was just too painful. To this day, Paul carries Seth's picture in his wallet even though we have never seen him since the day he placed our little boy in the mother's arms.

It does not matter how you lose a child, the impact and grief are similar. When someone says it feels like their heart was in their throat, that is accurate. My heart became so heavy it felt like there wasn't room in my chest cavity to hold it. The heaviness moved to my throat and even my extremities, weakening my entire body. I was fearful that my heart would implode, exploding on the inside from pressure, and yet wondered if that would bring some relief to the overwhelming state of heartbreak. My loss consumed my thoughts. Even when I was not thinking about it specifically, something would trigger a memory and the initial impact was felt once again. In the months that followed, every time I saw a new baby or watched a child playing, I would cry. I could not go down the aisle in the grocery store that sold baby food without breaking down. Every time the telephone rang, I was hoping it was her saying she had changed her mind. Days turned into weeks, then months, then years. I'll never forget our little boy.

Having survived another ordeal, I once again felt a bit stronger for it. My sister wrote me a long letter and tried to comfort me. "You must be very special people to have been through so much so young. There must be an extraordinary purpose for your lives and someday you will understand. I know you will help a lot of people who will draw strength from your experiences. You, too, will be stronger for having survived and it will help you as you go through life."

Although it didn't help much at the time, I have often thought of her words and they have been an encouragement to me. I comforted myself with the thought that someday I may be able to help someone else who had gone through similar experiences. I was still thinking like the minister's daughter even though the pain of the past couple years was often difficult. I would try to think positively and believed that it would get easier. Once again, my faith saw me through.

I was having a great deal of difficulty with painful menstrual periods. After seeing a specialist, I was diagnosed with endometriosis that was so severe I would have to be hospitalized almost every month for pain and hemorrhaging. It was excruciating and debilitating. I was also crippled with rheumatoid arthritis in every joint of my body. I was hypoglycemic and suffered with bouts of depression from all the medication I was taking. I also suffered with a stomach ulcer and had to watch my diet carefully. It was as if my body was falling apart. I knew that stress could play havoc on our bodies physically, emotionally and mentally. I am sure that was a good part of it. Yes, I was strong, but even as a young child was never in the best of health. All the stress was starting to take its toll.

My dream was to have a child of my own. The doctors told me that my slim chance of getting pregnant was to have surgery for the endometriosis. Over the next few years, I had three surgeries and after each one, I was no better than before. The hope of ever having a child was growing dim. Meanwhile, Paul underwent every conceivable test for fertility.

One day the specialist called us both into his office with a letter in his hand. We had no idea why he wanted to see us. We were sure it was some type of good news. Perhaps they had found a 'cure.'

We were secretly hoping he was going to tell us we were going to have a baby.

He began, "I am very sorry, but after all the testing and the surgeries, it has become abundantly clear. You are both sterile and there is not a chance in a million you will ever bear children." Just like that. He didn't try to soften the blow.

I couldn't look at Paul. I knew I would burst into tears. The hole in my heart was suddenly bigger. I thought it would swallow me up. My throat hurt. My stomach hurt. I heard little of what he was saying after that.

He told us to take his letter of recommendation to an adoption agency and get the ball rolling if we ever wanted to have a family. This news was insufferable. I just could not bring myself to accept it.

All I ever wanted was to be a wife and mother. Now I wondered if I would ever hold a child in my arms and call him or her my own. If we had known this when we gave Seth back, we may have fought harder to keep him, even realizing we probably would not have won.

Would I be able to convince myself to try adoption again? I supposed that Paul would be against it. The pain of this loss hit us both very hard.

Chapter Four

He was just sitting there, so very tiny, right in the middle of the intersection. But as I looked closely, I saw him quivering. I was appalled and astonished when no one stopped long enough for him to fly away. No one seemed to care. Cars from both directions drove right over him and each one just missed hitting him. I nearly drove over him myself and knew it was inevitable that he would die.

The adrenalin soared through me as I got out of my car in the middle of the intersection and raised my hands to stop all traffic. Horns were honking and people shouting obscenities from all directions, but my focus was not on them. I knew what I had to do. I had to save that little sparrow, and nothing else mattered.

Each step I took closer intensified my determination to save him. I bent down and gently picked him up and carried him to safety under a shrub on the corner. As I headed back to my car, instead of honking and cursing, I heard applause for my good deed. I felt exhilarated.

Then the strangest thing happened. I had a strong sense that

God was speaking to my heart. "How do you feel?"

"What do you mean how do I feel?" I thought. "Isn't it obvious? I feel wonderful."

I had a warm sense He was smiling at me, "Now you have an idea of how I feel when you fall down and I pick you up and take you to safety."

I was amazed. I had always beaten myself up for all the stupid mistakes I had made in my life and now it was like God was saying how much he enjoyed being there to help me, to protect me and to shield me. I never looked at God quite the same again. He truly loved me – I had no doubt.

Everyone has made mistakes or decisions that affect them in unplanned ways; some worse than others. People say or do things they regret but some mistakes have such lasting ramifications that they can affect someone's entire future.

Paul and I were about to make one of those mistakes. If we could turn back the clock, I wonder if we would have done anything differently. Would we have made the same decision? We will never know.

Our business was doing well and Paul was traveling a lot, which he thoroughly enjoyed. I managed the office and filled the void of motherhood with various projects. We bought a house in a bedroom community and settled into the suburban lifestyle. I stopped dwelling on the past and focused on the future.

We became involved in a small church, enjoyed many new friends, and were exceptionally close to two couples. The six of us socialized a great deal, both at church functions and other activities.

We had dinner together at least once a week, went ou

and thoroughly enjoyed each others company. We wei

to have made such good friends so quickly. We knew t

our business experience and asked a lot of questions. Much to our

surprise, the two couples approached us one evening and asked for

our expertise and assistance in setting up a jewelry store. They had

discussed this among themselves and decided it was a great idea and

would be profitable for all involved.

After a lot of discussion, Paul told them that he would help

them set up a store in downtown Vancouver and explained in detail

what would be required. We found an ideal location in an exquisite

heritage building in the hub of the city. Paul offered to do the

renovations himself to cut down on expenses and set to working out

the details. He agreed to put our business on hold and concentrate

fully on renovating the leased space to make it a first-class jewelry

store.

They said they had $50,000 to invest – was that enough? Yes,

we would be able to do a lot with that – both in making a beautiful

store and having adequate stock to get started. The whole deal was

sealed with a handshake.

We received the first installment of $6,000 per couple. Paul

had a knack at finding the best product for the best price and his efforts

certainly paid off. We were able to get the equipment we needed and

put a substantial deposit on diamonds and jewelry from our sources.

We had a good reputation with our suppliers and knew they would

give us merchandise on consignment with a small deposit.

When we were well into the construction and their deposit

austed, our new partners approached us once again. "We have decided not to go through with the store. It's taking far too long to get it up and running and we were expecting a return on our investment a lot sooner than this."

That was it. There was no discussion, no warning, they just changed their minds and were very unclear why.

"What do you expect us to do? We purchased all the necessary materials for the renovating and put deposits on the jewelry that we are committed to pay for. The jewelry we ordered from overseas is on the way here."

Paul and I didn't have the $12,000 they were demanding and it was our reputation on the line to our suppliers, a reputation we had spent a long time building. This was not the expected way to conduct business.

We had committed to the purchase; and if we did not pay the balance, the suppliers would keep the deposits. We tried to explain this to our friends but they didn't seem to care. They expected us to find the money somewhere and return it to them.

Old feelings from the past began to overpower me. It felt like another hopeless, unfair, and cruel scenario. The tension was mounting. They were adamant and would not listen to reason or give us any more time. We could not understand why they'd changed their minds.

Paul hated conflict and just wanted to resolve the situation quickly and painlessly. After much debate and arguing between the two of us, the only option we could see was to drive to the United States and sell as much of our inventory as quickly as we could. This would enable us to return our friends' investment and still save face with our suppliers. I was not in favor of this but really saw no other way out. We wrote and rewrote a long letter to our friends to explain our plans and to let them know we would be back as soon as we had the money.

We packed up and headed south leaving behind everything we had invested into getting the store up and running, including our own money and weeks of hard labor. Our goal was to return their investment, save the friendship and go back to doing what we were doing before they approached us with their idea.

We had no income and knew we had to move quickly so Paul started hitting the pavement, visiting all the jewelry stores, goldsmiths and suppliers from Nevada to California. I secured a job as an office manager in a hotel and enjoyed it. We settled in but it wasn't home. We worked hard and saved as much as possible to get us out of our jam and go back home.

It was really slow going. Most stores wanted to take merchandise on consignment and not pay for anything outright. It was a long process but we had no other alternative.

After three months of living like this, I was at work one morning when I received a phone call from Paul. His voice stammered when he said, "I only have a minute to tell you this. I have been arrested for two counts of fraud and being deported to Canada. You need to go home and pack my bag. I have 24 hours to go on my own volition or the authorities will take me back and it won't be pretty." Whatever that meant I did not know. I just knew that I was scared and angry and very confused.

My hands trembled as I walked into my boss' office. I swallowed hard to prevent my voice shaking and told him that I had a family emergency and needed to leave for the rest of the day. He looked right through me, and I felt like he knew what happened even though I knew he could not. He excused me and I drove home in a daze. I had more questions than answers. I couldn't think of anything he had done to warrant an arrest. It must be a terrible mistake.

Did I hear him right? This could not possibly be happening. Fraud? I didn't think so! If anything, I felt defrauded. Nothing made any sense. We tried to do what we thought was right. We had sacrificed so much to be in this position. We lost our business and our home in Vancouver and now this.

These two couples were our friends and they were Christians. I saw them as desperate people who were not thinking rationally. I also knew that they had no business sense but none of that made up for what they were doing to us.

Paul left the next morning while I stayed to pack and make all the necessary arrangements for the move back. I had to confide to my boss what happened and he was very understanding and sympathetic.

I would have to drive back to Canada with my loyal companion, our Sheltie, Perky. My extent of driving a long distance was about two hours. After that, I would have a strong tendency to fall asleep. At that rate it would take me a couple weeks to get back home.

A co-worker and I had become fast friends and I would miss her. When I told her what I had to do, she had a solution – a little white pill guaranteed to keep me awake. She gave me two of them and I didn't even question what they were – just wanted to get home as quickly as possible. I was still functioning in a state of confusion and disbelief. The whole situation was constantly in my thoughts. I kept asking myself why and how but came up empty.

I had packed the car to the headliner and above. Finally, I was on my way, but hadn't noticed how fast I was traveling. When I saw the police car's lights in my rear view mirror, it scared me. My nerves were too raw. With tears running down my cheeks, the officer still had no mercy on me and told me that because I was from out of state, the ticket had to be paid in the courthouse, not mailed. The courthouse was closed for the day and according to the state laws, I had to appear before a judge the next morning. I supposed that too many people never paid for tickets they received when they passed through. I decided to ask for a lesser fine when I appeared before the judge.

I had no place to go, a car full of everything I owned, and a dog. I would have to sleep in my car that night. After a couple hours of sleep, I went to the closest service station and tried to freshen up enough to make myself presentable for court.

I appealed to the judge who granted me a lesser fine and once again was on my way. Maybe the judge took pity on me because of the way I looked. In any case, I was glad to be on the road again.

After such an awful night of sleep in the car, I thought it would be a good idea to take the little white pills to make up for lost time. Within 20 minutes I was mustering every ounce of stamina to stay awake. They were not working. I rarely took medication but when I took anything, like a pain killer, it usually worked the opposite on me.

I barely made it to the side of the road and fell sound asleep.

I woke to the sound of a police officer tapping on my window and saying, "Lady, you can't use a public highway as a bedroom."

Luckily, I'd had enough sleep by then to get back on the road and keep trudging my way home. It felt like I would never get there.

I was oblivious to what was going on in Vancouver. I was also naive enough to think that everything would be resolved quickly.

When I finally got home, Paul told me that when his flight arrived at the Vancouver airport, he was met by plainclothes policemen and handcuffed like a common criminal. He was terribly shaken – emotionally and physically. He was taken to court and bail was set at $10,000. Paul had been granted one telephone call and called his uncle who put up the bail bond and he was released. His aunt and uncle were kind enough to allow us to stay with them for a few days until we found a place to live.

Hadn't we been here before? Alone, broke and abused by people we trusted? I knew many people would blame God at that point and wonder where he was but we knew God would help us through whatever mess we got ourselves into. Our hearts and motives were in the right place. We were very sorry for making such a stupid decision and just wanted to rectify it, make it all just go away.

"What are we going to do? Do you have any idea how serious this is? I just don't know if I am going to have the strength to get through it." I cried to Paul who didn't have any answers. Nothing made any sense. "Why did they go to the prosecutor and file criminal charges? Why wouldn't they just sue us for the money? Even if they won their case, they wouldn't necessarily get restitution." Paul tried to figure it out but came up empty.

After many hours of trying to determine what to do, we decided the only thing we could do was go back to the church, tell them it was entirely our fault and beg their forgiveness. We were fully prepared to pay them back every penny of their investment but we needed their forgiveness. Other than fleeing the scene in an attempt to make things right, we could not see what we'd done wrong. We had kept up our end of the verbal agreement but they hadn't seen it that way.

We remembered there was a meeting on Wednesday nights, so we decided to go with the hope of speaking to the two couples. We also knew the pastor, who was one of the man's fathers, would be there. Surely he would be reasonable and perhaps we could work out a payment plan or something to resolve the mess. We arrived a few minutes after the meeting started.

My feet felt deep-rooted in cement as we approached the church door. My legs were stiff yet shaking. It seemed as if I were 100 years old. Fear gripped me. I began to sway and Paul had to hold me up. I wondered how they were going to react and hoped they would accept our sincere apology.

"Don't worry," Paul assured me, "they will see that we meant them no harm and they will drop the whole thing."

Our only motive was to ask their forgiveness and receive adequate time to give them their investment back, even though our lawyer told us that we had no legal obligation to do so since fraud charges had been laid.

He told us this while chuckling, as if to say, "You would be getting off without having to pay them back." We saw no humor in that.

It took an eternity to walk to the backroom where the study

was taking place. A million times, I wanted to turn around and run back home. Even though I was so nervous, a part of me really expected them to welcome us with open arms. If the situation had been reversed, that is what we would have done. It was the right thing to do. It was the only thing to do, especially as Christians. I was hoping that this pain would all be over in a few hours and we could put the nightmare behind us. The first glimpse we got of them made my blood run cold. I have never seen such steely daggers for eyes. I started to sob and was barely able to compose myself for the duration of the study. The tension was so heavy and the air so thick it was difficult to breathe. They did not acknowledge us in any way.

Afterwards, the pastor asked us to meet him in his office with the two other couples. Surely, I thought, there they would listen to what we had to say and make peace. However, when it comes to money, people often change. We learned this then and continued to see it over and over throughout our lives. They really didn't appear to hear a word Paul said. I just sat there and wept. I was picking up on all the emotions flying through the room and it took every ounce of courage not to jump from my chair. I kept feeling faint.

"We have come here to offer you our apologies and full restitution," Paul explained. "It was never our intent to defraud you in any way, shape or form. When you decided you no longer wanted to be involved with the jewelry store, we thought long and hard on how to solve the problem, both with our suppliers and how to repay your investment." His voice was shaking as were his hands, but he continued. "Please recall that you were the ones who approached us and wanted to open a retail store with our help. We had no intention of opening a store until you asked us to help you do it."

The room was dead silent except for my sniffles as he continued. "We had explained to you before we left and also in the letter we sent you, we had invested the entire $12,000 in building materials, jewelry and deposits on product that would be sent to us upon total payment."

It was becoming evident they had one agenda and that was to see us suffer. They would not listen to reason. They would not bend. They were not hearing us.

"Please forgive us," begged Paul.

"We cannot forgive you" was the pastor's reply.

I didn't think I was hearing this correctly - a pastor who preaches mercy, telling us that he could not forgive us. It was the last I could bear. We stood up and extended our hands but they would not reciprocate. It was over. They wanted nothing to do with us.

"We'll see you in court," said one of the wives.

We could have so easily resolved the situation out of court, but not only did they insist on court, they went for the jugular – criminal court. Even criminal court would not guarantee them any restitution of funds. If they won, the only satisfaction they would get would be to send Paul to jail. It was quite apparent that this was what they wanted after they had been made aware of the facts from the prosecutor.

I didn't know which was worse--the possibility of losing everything once again, Paul going to jail, or losing faith in humanity -- Christians in particular. Too many emotions to sort through and my health was again at risk. The body can only take so much stress and mine was maxed out.

Because it was a criminal suit, they had the full resources of the Crown counsel - the best of the best. The prosecutor appointed to the case was a young aggressive attorney, busy making a name for himself. As far as we were concerned, our only financial option was to go to legal aid. The attorney appointed to our case was just out of law school, about as assertive as a snail, and not much brighter. I remember when I met him I thought, "Great! He has red hair. He will probably have some fire and fight in him."

He came to us misinformed of the facts and seemed uninterested. He offered no words of encouragement. He admitted this was his first criminal case and wasn't really sure what direction to take. He left us feeling like we were doomed before we started and knew we would have to do our own research and presentation of our case.

The court date was set for two years later and the process began. The police came into our home and seized all our records. We were not given copies of anything and were left with no documents or receipts with which to prepare our case. Our lawyer did little to help us. We found out later that he could have demanded we get copies of everything.

The accusations from our accusers started flying. One of the wives told the police in her statement that we promised them a $100,000 return on their $12,000 investment. Paul and I had promised no such thing and could not believe such nonsense. Now, it would be their word against ours. We had no proof – it had been a verbal agreement -- an agreement that was based on trust. A handshake.

We realized we did have one ace in the hole. A business associate, Andrew, had been with us when we discussed the store with our friends. We knew he would be able to testify on our behalf and confirm the details. He was our only hope.

When we told Andrew, he couldn't believe how we were being treated and assured us he would be there for us. He even offered us his safety deposit box to use for any valuables we needed to secure so the police couldn't confiscate them.

Andrew was a young man. He came from old money and his father was an extremely influential member of Vancouver business circles. We hoped his testimony would carry a lot of weight. Andrew found humor in the whole scenario and assured us over and over that there was no way this could happen. It was a simple agreement that went bad and would be rectified. "Happens every day of the week" he said.

The jewelry trade was a close knit group, much like a small community. It didn't take long for the rumors about us to manifest. We knew it would be difficult, if not impossible, to do any business until the dust settled. Paul had to hit the pavement and look for a job. He secured a job selling janitorial supplies to commercial businesses.

We had sold our car and anything else we could to pay back Paul's uncle the $10,000 for the bail bond. We were in a desperate situation, financially and emotionally.

We still had my old car but it was registered in the U. S. and Paul was not permitted to drive an out-of-country vehicle. So, my new job was chauffeur. Paul was given a few leads of existing clients but had a quota to meet by bringing in new business. We went to the industrial areas and I would sit in the car and read or stare out the window and think while he sold toilet paper. Demeaning and humbling, but we were thankful to have an income.

Each time he was able to secure a new client we got pretty excited as it would mean commission on future orders as well. Getting excited about toilet paper sales was a far stretch from selling jewelry, but it helped us to appreciate where we had been and look forward to where we were going.

It was getting more difficult for me to drive Paul everywhere and sit in the car all day so he decided to look for work at a car dealership where he would have a demo to drive. It would help his ego a bit to have a new showroom car to drive after being "in the pits" for so long.

Very quickly he was promoted to manager of a new Ford dealership in downtown Vancouver, and we finally seemed to be making some headway. Paul certainly did not want to stay in the car business the rest of his life but it was a means to an end, a decent income, and we were making some new friends. Once our case was resolved, we would get back into the gem business. We had lost most of our old friends – apparently they had been "fair weather friends" – and felt like we had little support.

Our lawyer was useless, too inexperienced, and immature so we had to do much of the research and groundwork ourselves. We were well into a year of preparation. We secured 25 character witnesses, many of whom were prestigious members of the business community, and we started to gain confidence that resolutions would come soon.

Throughout our ordeal, we continued to share in churches and youth groups wherever we were invited. We knew the church was where we belonged, and we would have done it full time if we could have afforded it. God had equipped us with gifts in many areas of service. Paul and I were not without faults, but we maintained the best attitude we could under the circumstances.

We knew from past experience and our upbringings that carrying a grudge, or worse, would be of no advantage. In fact, bitterness could cause ulcers and other health problems. We just wanted to do what was right, and get on with our lives. We needed to get past it.

We certainly had no intentions of hurting those who had the vendetta against us; we were only trying to protect ourselves. Our families were offering up a lot of prayer and gave us the support we needed. It was very difficult, especially for my father. He loved us dearly but after the mess of my first marriage and everything Joe had done, I often wondered how my dad processed all of these current events. But our families shared a strong faith and we believed with them that we would win our case or at worst, get probation.

Then the shock came like a demolition ball hitting my chest. With no warning, no note, no inclinations that anything was eschew -- Andrew committed suicide. The news hit us hard. I couldn't breathe. The pressure made my head feel like it was going to detonate. I screamed "NO, NO, this can't be happening. It just can't be true."

No one saw it coming. He had everything to live for and never seemed to be under stress. Grieving his loss was made worse when we realized, with his death, went our only witness and our only chance to prove our side of the story.

We waited ample time for Andrew's family to deal with everything involved and then approached them about retrieving our valuables from his safety deposit box. His father was completely uncooperative and unreasonable. He asked if we had any documents to prove the goods were ours and, of course, we did not. He was an extremely wealthy man and certainly did not need to keep our few gems.

It was becoming more difficult to maintain faith in the justice system but our lawyer kept assuring us, "You two have nothing to worry about. They have no proof of any fraudulent activity. It was just a business deal gone badly – happens all the time."

He strongly advised me not to testify. In case things did not go as planned, there was a chance I could be implicated as well. So, it was just Paul's word against four people with personal vendettas, whose motives remained a mystery.

"It really isn't fair, but you have to understand the way the system works. If the prosecution lies on the stand, it is not considered perjury. However, if the defense does, it could be devastating."

Was I hearing the lawyer right? Was he saying that our opposition was given a license to lie; but if we did, we could go to jail? He confirmed that was, in fact, the case. He explained that we were the ones on trial and the prosecutor would try to find anything he could to make us appear as liars. He would be watching and listening and try to trip us up in our testimony. On the other hand, if the prosecution's witness lied, it was regarded as a mistake and could be withdrawn. We had no intentions of lying and believed they would tell the truth as well. We hoped the trial would bring out all the truth and it would finally be over. We offered full restitution and knew that would work in our favor.

Paul's mother flew out from Alberta the night before the trial. It was wonderful to have her there to support and encourage us.

The morning she arrived our legal aid lawyer called. "I have been thinking about it and believe you should plead guilty. Please think about this carefully as you have a great deal of personal and business character references. You have no prior record. You can show that you can make full restitution."

Paul asked him if he was crazy. "We have been working for two years to try and prove our innocence and now you are suggesting I plead guilty?"

We argued with him but he did make a lot of sense. Paul would basically be saying he did it and was sorry and throw himself on the mercy of the court. We began to agree it was the best thing to do.

We had not seen our accusers since that Wednesday night. Two years had passed and we hoped there had been a softening in their hearts. Those hopes were quickly squelched when we saw them enter the courtroom. They appeared cold, hardened, and unapproachable. They brought an entire team of supporters who filled the courtroom, most of whom we had never seen before.

Our good attitudes faltered. We knew they had been hurt and felt justified in their actions, but we also knew we had not done anything wrong.

Mother and I sat in disbelief as we listened to lie after lie. "Paul promised us a return of $100,000 on our investment within six months" one stated.

Another was, "Paul and Carol approached us with an idea to open a jewelry store, but they did not have any money and wanted to borrow some from us."

The people we had considered friends told blatant lies and got away with it. Did they not realize what they were doing? They were possibly ruining our lives over a few thousand dollars that was offered back to them. Paul was painted as the worst type of con man. The person they were describing didn't even exist. I sat in my chair and wept.

Most of what was being said did not even register. Fear was my savior as it kept me from jumping up and screaming "LIAR! Why are you doing this?"

The pressure was such that I felt like I was going to have heart failure. It scared me even more because the room was starting to spin and there was a noise in my ears that sounded like thunder. I realized it was my heart beating but it was so loud I was sure everyone else could hear it as well. It was as if a vice was around my chest and someone kept tightening it. I was having more and more trouble breathing. Instead of easing up, it continued to get worse.

Our 25 letters of character reference were offered and read by the judge. Paul presented his case and then pled guilty, as advised. We broke for lunch.

Our emotional state was at a crucial point, but we continued to believe the judge would rule in our favor. He would see that we had in no way defrauded those people and yet were willing to pay restitution. Neither of us could eat lunch. I could barely hold down a glass of water. Paul's mother and our lawyer joined us and in light of everything that had happened in the courtroom, we were still confident. Lunch over; we made our way back.

The air was heavy with hostility and anticipation. I was in a cold sweat and couldn't even look at Paul for fear of bursting into tears. Mother noticed how arrogant our old friends looked. She was appalled by the whole ordeal and had a few choice words under her breath. I couldn't really hear what she was saying, but I know she was calling them names and was very ashamed of them to be acting like this in public when they professed to be Christians.

"Who do these hypocrites think they are? This guy calls himself a minister? He should be ashamed of himself. Someday he will stand before his maker and have to answer for this!" She whispered. Her words surprised but pleased me and I agreed.

"Please rise."

Paul stood in front of the judge to hear his decision. The pounding of my heart was so loud it was difficult to grasp what was being said. It was like I was in a cloud of smoke and nothing was understandable.

"Mr. Graham, I have read each of your character references carefully and have listened to the evidence provided. It is of my opinion that you are a man of character and good upbringing." It was wonderful to hear this. My fears quickly dissipated. It would be over once and for all. I could feel my chest pain easing.

The judge continued, "Yet you conned these people out of their money and need to be taught a lesson. I considered giving you a five-year sentence to the fullest extent of the law as a deterrent to others who might try something like this. However, taking your evidence into consideration, I have decided to only give you six months in jail."

"WHAT? No! This just could not be happening. I could not be hearing correctly. This isn't possible." I screamed in my mind.

The next few seconds were in slow motion. The floor became liquid beneath my feet, and I fell in a mass onto the floor and let out a scream that released all the bottled up emotions of the past few years.

The judge could have said six months, six years, or six decades. It really didn't matter, as any sentence seemed unfair and unbearable. Before the judge had a chance to complete his sentence, a shout of praise came from the cheering section of the courtroom. Those people were ecstatic. They had been vindicated. They stood and applauded. They cheered. They shouted, "Praise the Lord." They actually jumped up and down. They had won. They had seen justice.

If my mother-in-law had not been a Christian, I think she would have personally strangled each and every one of them right there in the courtroom. I gained enough composure to see the officer turn my husband around, place handcuffs on his wrists and lead him out.

What was I going to do? I couldn't go on. I had no income, no family near, and no friends. My health was rapidly deteriorating. But, more importantly, how was Paul going to cope? He was a gentle man. Jail was no place for him. I didn't know if he would be able to survive. I forced a smile and formed my lips to say, "I love you" as we exchanged glances and then he was gone. The door slammed shut behind him. I never felt so abandoned.

The smug prosecutor walked past me and said, "Don't worry about it – it will be over before you know it. He'll get steak every night for dinner."

I felt like saying "And maybe I'll be eating dog food, thanks to you!"

I wanted to punch him but I just stared at him and through the corner of my eye watched the victory party. I did not want to pay them back one red cent but I knew we would.   It would be the only way we could sleep at night -- but I wondered how our accusers would sleep.

Chapter Five

Six months! How did my husband land in jail? I didn't know any criminals. I didn't even know people who lived on the edge. I was a minister's daughter married to a minister's son whose foremost desire was to help people. Six months would be an eternity.

"Why, God? Did Paul have to go to jail to learn some incredible life lesson? Was this punishment of some sort? Are you angry with us? Why, God?" I felt like my questions fell on deaf ears and I felt even more alone.

We never expected Paul to go to jail. What were we going to do? I had no income and the lawyer informed us that Paul would be paid forty-nine cents a day during his incarceration. Actually, I didn't expect he would get anything, but, forty-nine cents a day? That was only $15 a month to pay for things like his toothpaste, chocolate bars, etc. Paul said he would send his entire check home to me. I laughed and cried at the same time. I did not know if I would cash it or frame it.

Paul's mother promised to stay with me for a few days so she could visit him before she returned home. I was relieved.

They sent him to Oakalla Prison. I knew he was going to jail but I had no idea it would be to such a hard-core place. Even so, I expected some form of cleanliness and order. I expected to see some normal looking people. I was so wrong!

On the way into the prison, Mother and I were confronted with a sign on the wall explaining what to expect. It stated that a physical search of all visitors would be made by patting the body with the hands and often by exploring body orifices in an attempt to find concealed weapons, explosives, drugs or other contraband.

To begin, we were body-searched. Then the contents of our purses were emptied and inspected. They removed my nail file and mother's rat-tail comb. They also threw away my package of gum and a candy mint. The room reeked of body odor, stale cigarettes, and worse, unrecognizable smells. The cement floors appeared to have been swept but they were still filthy. The walls were in dire need of paint. There was graffiti on them, phone numbers and obscenities. The last thing I wanted to do was to sit on one of the chairs. They were torn and dirty.

We were each given a number and told to sit down and wait. I felt queasy and worried I was going to throw up. I remembered reading about Oakalla in the newspaper. The city was considering shutting it down because of its poor safety standards. Guard supervision was inadequate. Cells in the basement, which at the time were used for solitary confinement, contained steam pipes that made living conditions intolerable, posed fire hazards for inmates, and were infested with rats. Maybe that was the other smell I couldn't figure out.

Conditions at Oakalla were decrepit especially the hospital area, which consisted of one section devoted entirely to active cases of tuberculosis, a first-aid office, a small room for violent and insane inmates, a dressing-room, a kitchen and an attic space filled with heroin addicts.

I said to Mother, "This is where my husband was sent. This is where our friends sent him. This is his new home."

We waited. It was so noisy. People were screaming obscenities at each other. People were arguing with the officials. Mother's eyes were opened wide as she took it all in. It was surreal. It felt like we were in a low budget movie. The plot was weak and we didn't really know what to expect.

"How do you think he will manage here, Mom?"

"I don't know, I just don't know." Mom was not prone to tears but they were welling up in her eyes and my heart went out to her in a new way. She was a strong woman who did not show her emotions. I never heard her say "I love you" as that would indicate a weakness. Now, I was seeing a softer side and my heart ached for her.

My number was called. I was afraid of what was to come as I was led into a room with a row of seats in front of a thick pane of glass. Each seat was partitioned to give a bit of privacy. I sat down and waited. Then he was there, sitting in the chair on the other side of the glass. We simultaneously picked up the telephone on our own side of the glass. I looked at him. His hair was greasy and awry. His cheeks were sunken in and he had a three-day-old beard. His eyes – it was difficult to look at his eyes. There were dark circles under them and they were dazed. His entire body was shivering. It wasn't that he was cold; I could tell he was terrified.

"Hi, honey!" I tried to keep my voice as calm as possible as I, too, was scared.

"Hi. I am so happy you could come. I wish you did not have to see me like this. Is mother with you?"

"Yes, she is waiting to see you."

"You can't let her know how bad it is in here. The two other guys in my cell are both murderers. I have not been able to sleep since I got here. I am even afraid to close my eyes. They gave me a filthy mattress to sleep on without a pillow or blanket. It is freezing in the cells and reeks of urine."

As he painted that word picture, my stomach turned and I felt sick again. I tried not to visualize him in that cell.

"Have you been able to eat?"

"No. I don't think I could even if they served decent food but what they are serving does not even resemble food. It looks and smells revolting."

By now, I was struggling to hold back the tears by biting my tongue and trying to figure out what I could do to help him.

"Please tell mother that it would be best if she didn't see me like this." Paul begged.

"You know I can't do that. She waited here to see you and I know she won't go home until she does. When she sees how bad it is, she will pray even harder for your release."

"I think they are going to move me tomorrow but I don't know where. My lawyer should be able to tell you." His voice was a bit steadier as I think I provided a temporary sense of security for him. I assured him that this, too, shall pass and we would somehow be stronger for having gone through it.

"TIME!" The guard yelled. I threw Paul a kiss and walked out.

"Hey whore, wanna good time?" "Spread 'em baby." I could hear the vulgar comments and whistles directed at me as I walked back into the waiting area where Paul's mother was sitting. My skin felt clammy and I was nauseated. I smiled at Mom as her number was called. Nothing had prepared either one of us for this. I knew her heart was about to be broken when she saw her baby boy. I held back the tears. I had to stay strong for her. I would have a good cry after she went home.

What had Paul done to deserve this treatment? He ran away from a financial obligation and ended up here. This would have been a natural time to feel hatred and revenge against those who put us in this position. But, thank God, that just did not happen. I knew what bitterness could do to one's psyche and health. It just wasn't worth it to carry a grudge. I had my moments of anger but knew I just could not go down that path. I wondered, sometimes, if we had used anger against our accusers, would we have won the case. We would never know. It didn't matter. What was done was done. I had bigger issues to deal with than to dwell on the "what ifs."

It was raining outside as we went back to the car. I took Mom's hand in mine and we walked in silence. I was glad it was raining. It felt like it was washing off the grime of that awful place. I knew I would not sleep that night and wondered if Paul would get any rest.

I could hear Mom praying in the room next to mine. I didn't want to close my eyes; because when I did, I just saw Paul's face and imagined him on that filthy mattress. I felt guilty for lying in a bed with clean sheets and a blanket. I wanted to cry but the tears were not there. I had a tightening around my chest. My stomach was burning and my whole body was quivering. Perky was never allowed on the bed but that night I called her and she jumped up and curled next to me. She licked my face and looked into my eyes as though she understood. It seemed as though she was asking me where Paul was and I just held her close.

Mom went home the next day. I was left with emptiness like I had never experienced before. How I wished my own mother was still alive. I wanted her to hold me.

When we came back from the U. S. we had to find an inexpensive place to rent. Our Vancouver house had gone into foreclosure. We ended up in Point Roberts, Washington. I had never heard of Point Roberts until we saw an ad in the paper for a trailer to rent. We had a look at it and decided to take it as the rent was only $200 a month.

Point Roberts is a geopolitical oddity that is part of the U. S. but not physically connected to it. It sits at the southernmost tip of the Tsawwassen Peninsula, south of Delta, British Columbia. It can only be reached by land from the rest of the U. S. by traveling through Canada.

It was not only unique but also tranquil. I felt a sense of security when crossing the border. There were about 300 residents, mostly vacationing Canadians. There was a gas station, a small grocery store, a post office, and several real estate offices. There was a large marina and many Canadians who purchased boats or yachts in the U. S., moored them in Point Roberts at a much lesser rate than they would pay in Canada. It seemed ideal, and we felt fortunate to find such reasonable rent.

Our landlords lived next door to our rented trailer. They were very kind, elderly people, and we sometimes played cards with them and had the occasional barbeque as neighbors often do. I knew I had to go tell them what had happened with Paul. I wasn't sure how to approach it, but I had to tell them I had no money but still needed a place to live.

My heart pounded as I crossed the property. I knocked on the door and they were pleased to see me. They invited me in for a cup of tea.

"I don't know how to tell you this without just coming out and saying it." I paused as I swallowed hard. "Paul was arrested and he is in jail."

The landlady cupped her mouth with both her hands and fell into her chair. "What happened? What did he do? Are you okay?"

All questions I really did not want to answer. I explained, "We had a business partnership go sour a couple years ago and instead of working it out in civil court, our partners took us to criminal court and shouted fraud."

"What do you mean? I do not understand. You are not

criminals!" Her heavy German accent came out strongly as she was getting angry at what she had just heard. "Who are these people? They should be punished!"

It felt great to hear these words from people we did not know that well but regarded us as friends. It made the rest of what I was going to tell them that much easier.

"I do not have a job right now and I have been quite ill. I will try to get a job as soon as possible and hope that you will consider being patient while I can get the rent together." My voice cracked as this whole concept was starting to become my new reality.

"Of course! Of course! Whatever we can do to help." They asked me to join them for dinner, but I just wanted to go home and cry. I had a lot to do and was baffled as to where to start.

I picked up the local paper and perused the classifieds. Right there in Point Roberts, the local grocery store was looking for a cashier. I knew the store owners and hoped the job was still available. Maybe I could get the job without having to tell them what happened. I needed to keep this a secret for as long as I could. I had enough to deal with without adding local gossip to the list.

I was feeling sick most of the time. I had dizzy spells and sometimes fainted without warning. I knew I needed to see a doctor but had no means to pay for it. My headaches were more frequent and I had a lot of abdominal pain. I knew it was more than stress – things just didn't feel right. I assumed I must be anaemic as my periods often lasted three weeks at a time and the first few days were unbearable – heavy bleeding and doubling over with pain. I tried to hide my concerns from Paul and would continue to do so. I hoped I would be able to hold down a job. I had to find a way to cope. I had no other options.

I planned to apply for the job the next day but first I had another dreaded task to do. I had postponed going to see Paul's boss, and I couldn't keep calling in sick for him.

Paul was sales manager at a downtown new car dealership, which entitled us to have a demo to drive. It would be difficult to return the car and tell his boss what happened but it had to be done, and quickly.

"Hi, Gary."

"Hi, Paul feeling better yet?"

I swallowed hard and continued. "Would we be able to go into your office to talk? There is something I need to tell you."

I could see the look of concern on his face, but he had absolutely no idea what I was about to tell him. He may have thought Paul was very ill or in the hospital.

"It is really difficult for me to tell you this but Paul is in jail." My voice was cracking as I explained in as little detail as I could what had happened and what the outcome was.

He put his head in his hands and shook his head. In a very quiet voice he said "But for the grace of God, go I. I am so sorry for you both and can only imagine how difficult this has been for the two of you. Is there anything I can do?"

I thanked him and told him I had brought the car back and appreciated his understanding. He told me to keep the car for a few days until I figured out what I was going to do.

The kindness of strangers is often greater than that of friends.

I so appreciated these efforts from people who didn't really know me. It helped me feel like I was going to make it through this awful ordeal.

It is amazing how fast you lose your friends when you husband goes to jail. People I had considered friends were not returning my calls. When I saw a close acquaintance on the street or in the store, they turned to avoid talking to me. So, I was alone. I even went to church alone. I didn't want to, but where else would I find any friends? I didn't have any money to go out and really didn't feel like it anyway. But I knew that I must socialize to a point in order to maintain some sense of sanity.

I remembered when my mother died my coworkers at the office treated me like I had the plague. Were they afraid that if they spoke to me, they might die as well? I never understood this concept. If a friend of mine was hurting, I couldn't get there fast enough. After all the rejection I had experienced, I never wanted to be one of those people who walked away from someone needing friendship.

Paul was granted one phone call each week and it was so good to hear from him.

"I've got great news. I will be leaving this hell tomorrow. I have been transferred to a work farm in the valley. You will be able to visit me there once a week. I have missed you so much I can hardly stand it another minute."

He was definitely sounding better. The farm was in Agassiz about an hour and a half drive from Point Roberts. Visitation was on Wednesday evenings.

I never remember being so excited. I wanted to look nice

for him but contemplating the environment I would be walking into, I certainly did not want to be leered at like I was at Oakalla. It seemed like such a ridiculous thing to worry about but I just wanted everything to be as good as it could be.

I was concerned about the drive out there. I had returned the demo to the car dealership as Gary requested, and the car I had was very old and not in the best mechanical condition. If it broke down, I would not have any means to fix it or an alternate way home.

Wednesday evening finally came and I allowed ample time to get there early. The farm was quite a ways off the main thoroughfare. It was dark out and I did not know the area at all. I managed to find my way and pulled into the parking lot. I was not prepared for what I saw. Most of the cars in the parking lot were worse than mine. Pretty rough cars matching pretty rough characters. The women and children who were lingering around the parking lot reminded me of street people I had seen in Harlem when I was in New York. I felt over dressed and nervous. But I didn't allow the scene to take away my excitement about seeing Paul. It had only been a little over a week but it felt like years.

It was a repeat of my trip to Oakalla. I don't know why I expected it to be different; false hopes, I suppose. I had hoped it would be middle class people visiting their husbands or friends who were white collar felons such as my husband. I assumed by their appearances that most of these criminals had committed drug-related crimes. A whole different world.

The doors opened for visitors to enter a building that looked a bit like a campground dining hall. I stood in line and waited my turn to be patted down and then to have my purse searched. I felt violated as visions of prison movies flashed through my mind. I realized this was routine to the other visitors. Many seemed to know each other and were joking and sharing stories.

We were asked to sit down at tables and then the inmates were allowed to enter. They were all dressed the same wearing two piece orange outfits that looked like hospital scrubs. Just like in Oakalla lot of whistles and vulgar comments were tossed in my direction but I paid no attention. I was looking for my beloved.

Then I saw him. He looked a lot better than the last time. He had a full beard and it was obvious he had showered. We embraced and then one of the guards yelled, "Hey, you two. No touching!"

We sat down across from each other at one of the tables. It was so noisy in there. At least half of the people were yelling. I tried to tone it all out and only listen to Paul. He shared what his days were like.

"We get up at 6:00 A. M. and breakfast is served at 6:30. We usually have oatmeal and toast and coffee for breakfast. They give us each a bag lunch and we board the bus to the job site."

"Is it the same every day?" I asked trying to sound interested in his new life.

"Yes, every day is exactly the same. We are working in the woods making cedar shingles. It means chopping down the trees, splitting the wood and making the bundles. It is hard labor and so cold and very wet."

"Do they give you adequate gear for working in the rain?"

"Not really and you get soaked to the skin by midday. There

are armed guards watching the men and the only break we get is 15 minutes for lunch. Lunch is usually a peanut butter and jelly sandwich and an apple."

"Look at this!" He showed off the muscles he was developing. "I never had any time to work out in the gym so I will really be able to get into shape here."

I tried to look and sound impressed but I just wanted to run away, screaming, "So this is what our lives would be like for the next six months!"

"Did everything work out okay with Gary?"

"Gary let me keep the car for a few days and I was also able to buy some time with the landlords." I assured him that everything was going to work out and that I would be starting my new job at the grocery store on the weekend.

The 45 minute visitation was over so quickly. We blew each other a kiss and said good-bye. I knew the next seven days would go by very slowly. It was pouring rain and very dark on my long trip home. I felt like crying but needed to see clearly while I drove. Crying would have to wait.

I started my job as a cashier and stocker for $1.75 an hour but only part time to start. I knew this was not going to be enough to pay my rent and living expenses so I found a second job cleaning house for a wealthy family. They paid me $25 a week, and I was so happy to be able to report this to Paul.

I could hardly wait until Wednesday night. Then Wednesday morning my car would not start. I knew it was more than a dead battery and didn't know what to do. One of the local mechanics came out and said I needed a new distributor cap but he wouldn't have one for a couple days. Was it only a couple years ago that we drove around in our new car and ate out almost every night? I broke down and sobbed.

"I'm sorry. Did you have somewhere special you needed to go? I really can't get the part any earlier," the mechanic explained.

"That's okay. I'll figure it out." I certainly wasn't about to tell him that I needed to go visit my husband in a work farm.

There was no way to get a message to Paul, and I knew he would be terribly worried when I didn't show up but there was nothing I could do.

The following week I left slightly earlier so the trip out to the farm would be in daylight. I was so relieved when I got there I felt like shouting "I'm here; I made it" but I just waited in my car until we were allowed inside. It was so good to see him and he was so relieved to see me. He looked much better again, even since the last time.

"What happened to you last week? I could hardly sleep thinking that you'd left me and I wouldn't blame you if you had." I never expected him to think that way but under the circumstances, I guess it was to be expected. I explained about the car.

"Well, I could hardly wait to see you to tell you my good news."

I expected him to say that he was going to be released but his idea of good news and mine were vastly different.

"The head of this farm has taken a real liking to me and he pulled me off of the work force in the woods. I got a new job cleaning the bathrooms and doing the laundry."

The thought of Paul being excited about doing laundry was pretty difficult for me to grasp, but I was thrilled for him nonetheless. It meant he could be indoors where it was warm and dry. Our visits were far too short and it was again time for the long drive home.

A couple of days later before getting ready for bed, I was getting out of the bathtub when I doubled over with pain in my abdomen. "What is going on?" I said out loud. Lifting one leg to step out of the tub, the pain grabbed me again. I reached for the towel rack to support myself. Carefully, I lifted my other leg and then leaned against the wall. I was alone and scared. Something felt terribly wrong. I tried to get to my bedroom but I was too dizzy and passed out on the floor.

When I came to, I could barely move but was able to crawl to the telephone and dialed the police. It was difficult to talk, my voice was weak. I asked them to send help. I knew my front door was unlocked and was grateful. I could not get to the door to let them in. They knocked on the door, and I knew they could see my lying on the floor, semi- paralyzed and very embarrassed because I did not have any clothes on. One of the officers threw a blanket over me as they were asking me questions.

"Have you taken any medication?" "Have you been drinking?" Have you used any illicit drugs?"

I explained that I had been going through a stressful time but that I was starting to feel better. Having them there gave me strength and with their help to get into my bed, I assured them I did not need to go to the hospital. They helped me into bed and told me to call them again if I had any more difficulty.

"Do you have any family or friends who could stay with you tonight?"

Having to answer "No" to that question just underscored my situation and I choked back the tears.

Perky sensed my fear and despair and cuddled with me in my bed. She gently licked my tears as they rolled onto my pillow. It only made me cry harder. I cried myself to sleep not knowing how I was going to make it through the next few months, not knowing what was wrong with me. I suspected stress was not my whole problem, but I could not afford to go to the doctor. I hoped that if I ignored it and pretended it did not happen, it would just go away. I hated being alone.

I went to work the next day because I could not afford to miss. I was hoping to get strong enough by Wednesday so that I would not have to tell Paul what happened.

The first thing he asked me was "Why are you so pale?" I told him I thought I might be coming down with the flu but knew I would be fine.

"The other day I was bending over a toilet to pick up the dirty bloody hypo needles that the drug addicts use in there. It is such an awful job and sometimes I almost cry when I think how I got here. But I had such a strong sense that no matter what has happened, God still cares very much for me. I know that vengeance is His and His alone! I am not going to question why this happened. Their unwillingness to forgive us for whatever they thought we were guilty of is not our concern."

We talked about how much we needed to maintain a good attitude and continue to trust God and thank him for everything he had ever done for us as well as everything he was about to do. Neither of us could ever hoard an unwillingness to forgive in our hearts. We knew it would only bear negative fruit.

Paul had more good news. He earned some day passes for good behavior. He was not allowed to cross the border to our home, so he asked me to arrange a place to stay in Canada to enjoy every moment we could have together.

On one such occasion we were at a restaurant and I wanted to show Paul something I had forgotten at home. I left him there alone for a few minutes while I went to get it. Paul had been placed in my custody and it had never occurred to me that a few minutes alone would matter. Apparently, it did. We had no idea that a detective had been assigned to us and was actually in the restaurant watching us. When I left Paul, the detective reported that fact to his superiors. Paul's day passes were revoked, his sentence was lengthened, and we would not be able to spend Easter weekend together as we had planned.

It felt like someone wanted us to mess up just to take away what little we clung to. After so many disappointments, it was hard to stay positive. I started to prepare myself for the negatives and began to focus on that. If I didn't expect much, I would not be as disappointed. I became a product of my own negative environment.

My health was rapidly deteriorating. I had saved up enough money to see a doctor, but he could not figure out what was wrong – he assumed it was hormonal. I was given strong medication with serious side effects. I was weak, nauseated, dizzy, and disorientated most of the time. Walking down the aisle of a grocery store one day, I collapsed and woke up in the emergency room. It scared me the first time it happened, and I was concerned about driving a car in case I blacked out. I tried to take extra precaution in everything I did so that I would not be in a life-threatening situation if I passed out again. I tried to recognize the signs before it happened and to put myself out of harm's way. I had to hide this from Paul as it would worry him.

We continued appealing Paul's extended sentence, and he was finally released after six months. In the course of a lifetime, the time he served was a mere moment yet it had seemed forever. The separation took its toll on each of us individually and as a couple. It would take time to heal the wounds and get back on track. I blamed him for making the mistake in the first place. I was angry at myself for not following my instincts and putting my foot down about not going to the U.S.

He was given a temporary visa to live in Washington with me. We settled into enjoying small town life instead of living in fear and apprehension. We did the best we could to put the past behind us.

My monthly periods were getting worse. The pain was so intense my entire body would become contorted and I could not walk at times. My hands would twist like a pretzel. It was like my entire nervous system seized and I lost all control. The pain was unbearable. Paul had to carry me into emergency regularly to get some relief. Thoughts of my mother's suffering were plaguing me as I began to wonder if the same thing was happening to me.

I continued to see a specialist and was put on various

medications. Then I got the phone call from his office asking me to come in as the doctor had a diagnosis. That conversation has been seared into my psyche. I will never forget any part of it. It changed my life. The doctor just stared at me, and then glanced around the room. I was feeling uncomfortable and didn't know if I should speak or remain silent. I chose the latter. Seconds felt like minutes and then he spoke. There is one word in any language that is difficult to hear. It immediately brings fear, guilt, anger, and an assortment of questions. Why me? How did this happen? It is an ugly word. That word is -- cancer.

It rolled off his tongue far too easily. I could not form my lips to mutter it. My mother had died of cancer. I was a young woman in my twenties. I was trembling and frightened.

"Carol, basically you have two choices and I think it is obvious which one you will choose!" I assumed he meant two types of treatment. He continued, "Your choices are hysterectomy or death." He paused for impact. "You are a very sick young woman." He seemed far too nonchalant about the whole subject, very matter of fact.

I thought this was rather crude. How could he be so insensitive? In hindsight, it is probably a good thing he was this way – it made me angry and I responded in like manner. Strength I did not know I had welled up inside of me and I said "I do not accept those choices. There has to be another way! I will find that alternative."

I might as well have told him that he was ugly or stupid or both. Rage overcame him. I had challenged his intelligence. He was a learned doctor; a specialist in good standing and a young uneducated woman was telling him she did not accept his opinion as fact. He rose up from behind his desk, leaned over it towards me and pointed his finger in my face. He was so angry he was shooting spit when he said, "Well then, lady, go home, suffer and.......die!"

It was as if my life flashed before my eyes. All the struggles and trauma of my past gave me supernatural strength. That strength began to rise up within my inner most being and I knew I would fight this battle and win. There came a sense of peace and assurance that this was NOT the end – it was merely another beginning. There would be a miracle. I had no doubt.

I stood up, spun on my heel and started out of the room. Then I paused, turned, and said in a loud staccato voice, enunciating each syllable clearly. "I... will.... walk.... in here.... pregnant.... one day." I couldn't believe the words that came out of nowhere. But in my heart, I knew they were true and I challenged myself to find a solution to my health problems. I was through being battered and I was going to succeed. Nothing was going to stop me. I almost screamed out loud "ENOUGH, not this time."

I weaned myself off all the medications and decided that if I was going to get any help at all it would be divine. The medical profession had failed me miserably and gave me little, if any, hope. Hysterectomy – I didn't think so. Death – not my time yet.

I knew that God had to have an answer for me and I was determined to find it. I remembered my father telling me how I almost died as a baby. That same faith my parents had for me began to build up inside and confirmed that I would be victorious in this conflict.

I knew that God would heal me and give me the child I had longed for all my life. Sometimes, on the rough days, it was more difficult to believe. But, there was a seed planted in my heart and the more I nurtured it, the stronger it became. I remembered my father teaching me that whatever you feed will have a tendency to grow and whatever you starve will have a tendency to fade and die. I could feed my fears or feed my faith. The choice was mine. I chose to keep that promise in front of me, feed my faith and never forget in the dark what I had seen in the light.

The weight of the diagnosis hung over me. My anger in the doctor's office turned to frustration and anxiety. I knew I was going to be okay but how would I get there?

About three weeks after I had seen the doctor, an acquaintance of mine called. She was representing a company called Shaklee and said she was giving a food supplement demonstration in her home and was wondering if I was interested. She knew that I had been very ill and thought it could help me. I told her I would attend but only to support her. I really had no interest in food supplements. I had been taking vitamins faithfully and they weren't doing me any good as far as I could tell.

I attended the meeting and was amazed at all the information the woman had to offer regarding our food and how it was processed. It was all relatively new information and went against the general rule of thought, which was that we could get all our necessary nutrients from the food we consumed.

The more I listened, the more hope I felt. No doctor had ever given me hope for improvement. They just continued to alert me as to how things would get progressively worse. Could this be my answer?

Then she hit me with a statement I will never forget. "If you do not get results, you get 100% of your money back. No questions asked!" Was I hearing her correctly? First I had hope and now a money-back guarantee that I would get results.

At that time, Shaklee sold eight different food supplements. She explained what each one was for and I bought all eight. I had nothing to lose and possibly everything to gain.

I took my bag of hope home and Paul said "I bought some of that stuff years ago but never used it. Just bought it to be nice to somebody." He was surprised I'd spent so much money and guessed it would end up sitting in the cupboard eventually ending up in the garbage.

The next day I started my new regime of food supplements. I was excited and anxious. Three days later, I sat down and wrote a Thank-You card to the woman who had done the demonstration. I wrote "Thank you" about one hundred times and signed it. I could not believe that I could feel this good in less than a week. Even if I never felt any more improvement, it was worth my investment to feel this good for a few days. That simple little house meeting I attended started me on a whole new road of health awareness. It became my passion that has sustained me for over 40 years.

I researched each product and took every course I could find about various food supplements and how they worked. I was determined to improve my health and there was no doubt whatsoever that God had directed my path. I promised myself and my doctor that

I would walk in there pregnant one day. I had new confidence that I most definitely would do just that.

Chapter Six

Paul and I wanted to start a family but knew we needed help. I was convinced that we would have children and with my health improving I saw great potential in fulfilling that dream.

We both started individual therapy. Paul was put on Clomid in hopes of increasing his sperm count. I had three surgeries for endometriosis. After each surgery, my pain would lessen for a few months and then return. It seemed like an uphill battle and nothing was producing the positive report we had hoped to get. It was difficult to convince Paul to think about adoption. He did not want to watch me go through the pain of disappointment in case things did not work out. My arms ached to hold a little one. My heart longed to love a child of my own.

"I want the two of you to seriously consider adoption." My new doctor must have read my mind and hearing those words from a specialist helped convince Paul that adoption was the way to go.

"You are both in your mid-thirties and your chances of having a baby placed with you are getting slimmer. Agencies tend to place babies with younger couples. It would be easier if you already had children or were willing to adopt an older child." His words were depressing.

I began researching our options; but each time I picked up the telephone and called an adoption agency, I became more depressed. "I am sorry but we are not accepting applications at this time," was the constant response. The waiting list with any public agency was a minimum of five years. It seemed hopeless. My dream was hanging by a thread.

Then someone told me about an adoption agency in Seattle, Washington. They encouraged young teenage girls not to have abortions. Instead, they supported the mothers, helped them through their pregnancies and had them consider adopting out their babies. My hopes were high and I could hardly dial the number to set up an appointment. My hands were shaking. I wanted this so much and the thought of rejection was making me hesitate. My emotions were all over the place but I made the call.

Although it felt like a major step in the right direction, I was terrified of facing another disappointment. I knew my age and my health history would work against us. What I didn't know was how thorough their investigation would be and what would happen if they discovered my husband had a criminal record. I felt defeated before we started, but I had to try.

One thing in our favor was that we purchased a home in Point Roberts. Considering everything that had been working against us for so long, our home purchase came far easier than we had ever imagined. We saw it, we liked it, and we bought it in the hopes of it helping our chances to adopt. It all fell into place within 24 hours.

Before the adoption agency interview we needed to complete a book of forms. It seemed like an endless process. I realized if all prospective parents went through the same scrutiny that adoptive parents did, there would be a much greater understanding of the seriousness of child rearing.

We individually submitted letters from specialists stating we were "sterile without any chance of conception." We also had to have credit reports and criminal record checks done. We were relieved to learn that our past experiences had not affected our credit rating. Our other concern was Paul's criminal record; but we had applied for and received a full pardon from the Canadian government as soon as he was eligible.

We went through a long process to obtain letters of reference from professionals, (banker, lawyer, minister). We also had to submit personal letters of reference from people who had known us for a number of years and from family members. They required no less than 15 letters of recommendation.

We each had to complete an autobiography, which was to include our childhood and family lives, and current relationships with our parents and siblings. We needed to share important events in our lives as children, teenagers and as young adults. Our educational backgrounds and work histories were taken into consideration. They wanted to know our current activities, interests, and lifestyles. We each had to describe our marriage and our spouse in various scenarios.

Then they wanted us to write about the emotions we felt when we were told we were not able to bear biological children. Why did we want to be parents? What were our attitudes about child rearing and discipline? And finally, what were our life goals and hopes?

After all these forms and reports were considered carefully, we were granted a home study to be sure our home was perfect for the new addition. Personality traits and habits were questioned. In-depth interviews were conducted individually and together asking about our strengths and weaknesses and how we would handle different situations. Throughout the investigation, the tension was high. Would we pass the test? Would I mess up and miss my chance of being a mom? What would we do if we were turned down? Would I be able to take any more disappointment before reaching a breaking point? Then the waiting game.

A few days passed and I assumed the worst. The adoption was constantly in my thoughts. I would go over and over the interview and the letters of reference and wish I had said this or not said that. The days turned into weeks and I became more depressed. My sleep was disturbed by fear of never being a mom, and I would cry during the night at the thought. I wanted to call the agency but was concerned that it might ruin my chances by sounding over anxious and concerned. Months passed. I had little hope left. It became difficult to believe God would grant us our desire.

I will never forget the day the letter came. I saw the return address and my hands were shaking so hard I could not open the envelope. I ran into the house screaming "Paul, we got the letter! Come quickly!"

Paul ripped it open and read "We are pleased to inform you that you have been accepted as candidates for adoption." I almost passed out from relief. Falling into the closest chair I began to laugh. The worst was over.

One month went by, then two. Three months, then four. Why wasn't our baby miraculously appearing? We passed the test, what was the hold-up? Another month, then two more.

Meanwhile, well-meaning friends would comment on our situation.

"Are you sure you want to go through with adoption? I thought you said that God was going to heal you and give you a child of your own." I wanted to answer them and ask if they ever walked in my shoes. Did they know what it felt like to be childless and wanting nothing more than to have a child?

"Maybe you just imagined you were going to be healed. Maybe you will never have children." I wanted to tell them to keep their doubts to themselves and not inflict them onto me.

"I thought you told the doctor you were going to walk in his office pregnant someday. Don't you still believe that?"

Their words only added to my anxiety. It felt so very right to try and adopt a baby who needed to be loved. I knew we would love him or her as our own. Besides, I hoped to have more than one child and still believed I would bear a child someday.

It was nine months to the day after we had been accepted when the phone rang.

"This is Maria with the adoption agency. I have some news for you." She didn't say it was good news. Were we being rejected for some reason? Had they changed their minds? The tension was unbearable!

"We have a baby for you. The mother is in labor and should be giving birth very soon. We will keep you posted." She was quite matter of fact about it. They placed so many babies it probably was standard procedure for her. I guess she had no idea how anxious I had been for so many months.

I fell to my knees. It was really true. It was really happening. I was going to be a mommy. We were going to be parents. All the past hurts disappeared; they didn't matter. My greatest desire was being fulfilled. No one could ever take the joy away that I felt at that moment.

I could hardly dial the phone to call Paul, my father, my sister, and everyone I could think of to tell them the wonderful news. My head was spinning uncontrollable. I didn't know what to do first. The baby's room had been ready for over a year, but I needed to do last minute preparations.

The first call had come on Tuesday. On Thursday, we got the news we waiting for.

"You will be able to pick up your son on Monday."

YOUR SON! OUR SON! I loved the sound of that – *OUR SON.* Our little boy. Our pride and joy. Our first-born.

I still believed we would also have a baby girl someday; but right now, we were going to have a son. The chances of us adopting two children or giving birth twice were very slim. This was perfect – there was no doubt whatsoever in my heart.

Sleep was out of the question. My mind raced with excitement making sure everything was ready for the baby. I had researched baby formulas and decided I would never use them. I learned the best alternative to mother's milk was goat's milk and I had to find a trusted source.

My niece recommended a magazine article that showed how adoptive mothers could actually nurse their babies using a Lactaid. This was so exciting. I ordered all the necessary paraphernalia and stocked up. I never understood why women who could breastfeed naturally sometimes opted out of that pleasure, that bonding. I couldn't wait to nurse my firstborn, my very own baby boy and create an everlasting bond with God's gift to us.

I kept telling myself to get some sleep knowing the next few months would mean sleepless nights but I just couldn't. I had waited all my life for this occasion. There was so much to think about - plans, lists, shopping.

Finally it was Monday. We woke early to go pick up our son. All the last minute preparations were done. My house was spotless. What difference that would make to a newborn, I did not know. But nonetheless, it was important to me.

The telephone rang. I wasn't going to bother answering it as we were headed out the door to pick up our son, but decided I should.

"Carol?"

"Yes"

"This is Maria."

"Yes"

"I am afraid I have some bad news for you."

I sat down. No, it just could not be. This could not be happening. I thought if only I had not answered the phone, it would have been all right. Tears flowed fast and easy. She didn't need to say anymore. I couldn't bear to hear it.

"The birth mother has decided to keep her baby. I'm really sorry Carol. The choice is hers and there is nothing we can do. I am sure we will find another baby for you soon."

Another baby? I did not want another baby. I wanted my baby, my son.

I remembered what my 'friends' had said. Was this not supposed to happen after all?

The next three months were agony. Every day I wondered if it would be the day. Doubts ran rampant as friends continued to feed me negative thoughts. My faith was wavering. My spirits were low. Maybe I had been wrong.

We found out much later that the birth mother had actually adopted that baby out when he was six months old and then took him back three months later. That poor child. Also, I could not have imagined how it would have felt to have had him for six months and then to lose him. I don't know if I would have been able to cope. Only God knew I would not have been able to go through that again and he spared me from all that pain. He always knows best even when we think we know better!

Just when I thought I was starting to get over the pain, the phone rang.

"Carol"

"Yes"

"This is Maria."

Now what? I thought.

"We had a couple come into our office a few months ago;

and when they walked in, we all looked at each other and could not believe our eyes. The baby's father could be your twin brother and his name is the same as your husband's – Paul. It was phenomenal. We knew this was your baby. He was born two days ago. Would you be able to pick him up tomorrow?"

Be able to pick him up tomorrow? Heaven and earth couldn't stop me. Paul was out of town speaking at a youth conference in Seattle. I would get the news to him, and we would meet Maria from the agency tomorrow. I was ready to park myself on the hospital steps and steal him if I had to. I was NOT going to lose this baby. My baby.

They told me later they hadn't wanted to get my hopes up prematurely by telling me this was in the works. They decided not to say anything until they knew for sure to prevent my getting disappointed all over again.

"There is a slight problem, Carol. The grandmother does not want to allow the adoption and she has threatened to harm anyone trying to take the baby out of the hospital. It would be best if we meet at a place that no one knows but us." It scared me but I wasn't going to say no.

We decided to meet in the parking lot of a large Catholic church on the highway. Paul and I arrived much earlier than the appointed time. We sat there. We paced the parking lot. We tried to prepare ourselves for another disappointment but, at the same time, thinking positively.

"What is taking so long? Something must have gone wrong. Where is my baby?" Paul tried to reassure me but I kept asking, "Do you think this mother changed her mind? Maybe they couldn't get out of the hospital without causing problems with the grandmother."

Maybe, maybe. What was taking so long? Where was he? A car approached the parking lot very slowly. The driver was a woman looking for something. "Look, look, right over there. That has to be her."

Excitement quickly turned into fear, "There is no baby, NO BABY, just the driver."

I jumped out of the car in disbelief; but as I approached, I realized I could not possibly have seen the little car seat in the back. "He's here! He's here! He's so tiny. He is looking at me."

I had never seen such a small baby. I held out my shaking arms. "Carol, until I officially hand him over to you, you may not carry him. I will carry him into the church, and we can do the paperwork there."

"Paperwork? Please just give me the baby!" I thought.

It was a busy place. Priests and nuns and other people were walking around. No one knew why we were there and no one asked. We just walked in as if we belonged. Maria chose a room. We followed her in and closed the door. She undressed our son and showed him to us.

"Please inspect your son."

"Inspect our son? What am I supposed to look for?" I was thinking that maybe something was wrong with him and they wanted to see if I could find it.

"Just make sure he has all his fingers and toes. You don't have to take him if you do not want him."

"Are you out of your mind?" I almost shouted. "This is our child. He was meant to be our child. How could you possibly suggest we not take him?"

"Please look at him and be sure he is okay." Maria continued.

He was perfect – a lot smaller than I had expected but actually weighed seven pounds, two and one half ounces. She proceeded with the paper signing and gave us a "welcome" package of diapers, formulas, etc.

I thanked her but blurted out "I will not be using the formula under any circumstances." Oh no, I thought. Will she think I'm an unfit mother not knowing what is best for my child? Will she take him back unless I feed him formula? But my fears were short-lived as she handed him to me.

I wasn't sure how to hold him. I was afraid he might break. But nature took over very quickly and my fears were soon replaced with the assurance that this was what I was always meant to be - a mommy.

Maria told me he had been spitting up a lot and didn't seem to like his formula. I amazed her by pulling out my prepared goat's milk, which he welcomed. I held him in my arms to feed him and we made eye contact. The moment our eyes met, it was love - unconditional, everlasting love.

Paul had to go back to the conference, and I went along to show off our new son. Our dear friend, Father Chuck, blessed him, and we cried as the truth of the moment began to sink into our hearts. We were parents. This was our son. His name was Jason Paul. We could not have been prouder.

On the long drive home, Jason stared at me the entire time. I didn't know a newborn could stay awake that long. I sang to him. I talked to him. I cried. I pulled the car over to the shoulder several times just to hold him, touch him. He was perfect. He was mine.

The agency had warned us that the birth mother had six months in which to change her mind. If all went well, we would attend a hearing with a judge and he would sign the final papers. Then Jason would be legally ours. In the meantime, we were on borrowed time.

We were not sure how to cope with that kind of pressure. Were we not supposed to love him for six months, just in case we had to give him back? Now we faced another six months of waiting, but as each day passed, I knew he was never going to go away. He was ours.

The day finally arrived. We went to the judge's chambers. I will never forget and never understand why the judge, sitting across his huge desk, was wearing a ridiculous black and white polka dot bow tie that measured shoulder-to-shoulder and about eight inches wide. Was this a ploy to make us feel comfortable? Whatever it was, it worked because my tenseness lifted, and I had to restrain myself from bursting into laughter.

He was saying things like "You realize, I am sure, that this is not a child you can have for a little while and then give away if you don't want him. This isn't for a year or ten years or even eighteen years – this is for life."

Was he kidding me? This was what I had waited years to hear. No one, nothing, nada was going to take away my son. God had planted him in our hearts and our love for him would only grow

– no matter what!

I was not thinking ahead to the frustrations parenthood would surely bring. All I thought about or could see was the absolute innocence and beauty of that baby in my arms and in my heart. Surely this was the greatest gift anyone could give. The greatest gift God could give us. I thanked Him every day for the mother who gave him life and loved him enough to give him to us to love and care for him as our own.

At the time of the adoption I was working at a jewelry store. As much as I wanted to be a full-time mom, I knew I had to work to help with expenses. The adoption had been very expensive and even though we had borrowed money to help us get through, we still owed a lot of past debt.

A dear friend of mine offered to take care of Jason. I knew he would be in good hands; but all day at work, I thought of him and longed for the day when I could be a full-time mom.

Friends and strangers admired him, asking, "Have you ever seen such a beautiful baby boy?" He was perfect in every way. I never expected to be so blessed with such a wonderful child. And he was ours. Forever.

It was almost Christmas and I was excited about going back home as soon as possible to introduce our son to his grandfather. I had waited so many years for this and knew my dad would be a wonderful grandpa to Jason. Then, a few short weeks after Jason was born, my father called unexpectedly to tell me, "I have been diagnosed with cirrhosis of the liver, just like your mother."

How was this possible? I could not lose him now. Neither

one of my parents had ever consumed alcohol in their entire lives. After my mother died, an autopsy determined that her condition was a result of hepatitis she had contracted as a young girl. Now, I was wondering if she had passed it on to my father. This wasn't fair. I was determined not to accept it and hoped it was not true.

I was just starting my family. I needed him. My son needed a grandfather. My dad was a man of incredible faith. He had seen so many miracles in his life; and he believed, without doubt, that he would be healed and made whole. We stood with him and agreed this was not the end.

Jason and I flew out to visit him, and it grieved my heart to see my dad looking so thin and unwell. He had always been a picture of health. He exercised every day and was rarely sick with a cold or flu. I agreed with him that although he was only 78 he could easily live to at least 100.

I always hoped that when I had a child my father would bless him in a church ceremony. So, when Jason was six months old, Paul and I took him back home for the occasion. It was the fulfillment of my dream. To have my father pray the blessing on our son was one of the most wonderful and memorable days of my life. I did not, however, expect it to be the last day I would see my dad.

But it was. Although I was not living in the area, my father and sister kept me informed of his deteriorating condition. He went downhill rapidly but continued to maintain a positive attitude that he would recover. I kept encouraging and agreeing with him but in three short months, he was gone. Two days before he died I called him. He was in the hospital and a nurse held the phone for him.

"Hi Daddy." I desperately tried to maintain a steady voice. There was no response from the other end of the phone, but I could hear him breathing heavily.

"I just wanted to tell you how much I love you and how much I appreciate everything you have done for me."

His breathing seemed louder, and I assumed he was getting emotional. "I am going to see you again someday, in heaven. Please tell mother, when you see her, how much I love and appreciate her as well."

It was so difficult for me to continue "Thank you, Daddy, for the way you raised me. I will be grateful for you forever." He was too weak to respond but it was wonderful to have the opportunity to say good-bye.

Then he was gone. Just like my mother — both gone. I felt numb.

But what he left me was a heritage of strength and courage. He taught me to "Do it right. Do it now." He taught me never to procrastinate. He taught me to "search for God" in everything I did. He taught me that if I stumbled and made mistakes, "God was there to pick me up and lead me." I think one of the most important things he taught me was how to forgive. I am forever grateful.

My middle name was Jean, and I don't ever remember him calling me Carol. In fact, when an insurance salesman came to our house when I was a girl, he asked for my full name and my father couldn't remember it. He had to ask me. We all laughed.

I missed his weekly phone calls. He used to wake me every Saturday morning around six o'clock. "And da Jeannie. And da little honey." His German accent was strong and it was a wonderful sound to wake up to and start my weekends. It was the same song he sang to me when I was a little girl. I loved our regular chats and there was a huge void in my life when they stopped. I miss him so.

I was in the habit of depending on my father's prayers and believed that when he prayed for my situations, everything would turn out right. Depending on him took the pressure off me. It had been my crutch and now I was without that support. I had placed more faith in my father's prayers than I did my own.

It was like getting kicked out of the nest. I would now have to stand on my own two feet and seek my own answers from God. I was out of my comfort zone and into a new learning process. It would take time.

Chapter Seven

It seems no matter how old we get, we are always eighteen and waiting for our lives to begin. My dreams of a normal life were finally being fulfilled. There wasn't a white picket fence, but we had a comfortable, cozy home with a beautiful yard. We were now a family. Paul had, once again, established himself in the gemstone business and was wholesaler to the trade. He leased office space in Tsawwassen, just north of the Point Roberts border in Canada. Life was good.

We made friends with a couple in our neighborhood and it was nice to be social once again. They were renting their house and when it came up for sale, rather than move, they decided they would like to buy it. They were not in a financial position to do that so Paul offered to work out a trade with the owner using gemstones as a down payment. In return, we would own a half interest in the house. We had the paperwork drawn up and for two years everything went as planned.

At the end of the two years, the owner who had been carrying the mortgage demanded to be paid out. The only way our friends could get a bank mortgage was as sole owners. We knew, only too well, what it was like to be in a desperate situation so we helped them out by signing our portion over to them with the understanding that we were still half owners. We were all happy with the arrangement; but soon afterwards, they were unavailable to have dinner or play cards with us. They kept making lame excuses, and we began to feel they were avoiding us. When we realized exactly what they were doing, we confronted them. They informed us it had been their understanding that our portion was gifted to them, and we no longer had an interest in the property. Once again, we both felt betrayed and ignorant. The relationship with them was over.

"What I just don't understand is when we seem to be doing the right thing and are nice, people take advantage of us." I confided to Paul.

"That's human nature," Paul had told me more than one time, "just let it go, there is nothing we can do to change it." He always seemed to know what to say to give me the strength and understanding I needed.

Midst all the turmoil, it was wonderful to have our son in our lives. He brought us such joy. Shortly after Jason was born, I decided to quit my job at the jewelry store and be a full-time mom. It meant tightening the belt a bit but worth every sacrifice. I enjoyed all aspects of homemaking, from housework to playtime. It was what I always wanted and I was not disappointed. I forgot about all the years of struggling to have a baby and all the doubts and frustrations involved with that. Jason fulfilled so many areas in my life and I loved every moment of motherhood.

Jason was an incredibly happy little boy. He was very content and well behaved. We took him everywhere we went. Whether it was a restaurant or church, he was a pleasure to have with us. I had not carried him in my womb, but I carried him in my heart and he won the hearts of everyone who came in contact with him. People often commented how much he looked like us. I would thank them and never let on that he was adopted. It made me so proud. No child could have been loved or wanted more.

Jason was 18 months old when I opened a kitchen drawer and found a nest of eight of the tiniest baby mice. I felt faint, let out a horrendous scream and slammed the drawer shut. I got up on a chair and was starting to climb on top of the kitchen table. The idea of those little filthy creatures in my home, my kitchen, my drawer was unthinkable. As little as they were, they appeared huge as they were in control of my emotions, and I didn't know what to do about it.

Within a micro second Jason was in the kitchen. With all the sincerity and composure a child of 18 months could muster he ran to my aid, patted my knee and said "It's o tay, Mommy. It's o tay." Then he proceeded to open the drawer and carefully picked up the first mouse. I wanted to scream at him "Don't touch them, they are gross." But instead I watched in awe as he carried each of the eight miniature mice outside. He placed them in a secure place in the same little nest mother mouse had made for them. I had a much better idea of what to do with these creatures, but I was too stunned to say anything as I watched my little saviour come to his mother's rescue.

My health was gradually improving. I was noticing various symptoms disappearing. My periods were regulating, I slept better, and pain levels were going down. I had energy! The crippling arthritis that inflamed my joints was gone. The doctor's cursing words lingered in my ears; but I knew one day, I would be totally and completely healed. It was just a matter of time.

I took some courses and read everything I could to learn about total health and nutrition. I became certified as a Symptomologist, trained to analyze symptoms, which are alerts to other problems or deficiencies. I learned that masking symptoms, which drugs often do, will not repair, or correct the problem. Feeding the cells the nutrients they require for repair will aid the body to heal itself. When the problem is corrected, the symptoms are naturally alleviated. It made pure, logical sense, and I began to share the concept with friends who had seen the great improvement in my own condition. The same passion I felt in the doctor's office when I told him I would return pregnant grew stronger every day.

On one bright sunny day I ran some errands in our brand new Ford pickup truck. I was doing about 35 miles per hour when, without warning, my steering wheel locked. The truck was totally out of control; and in a matter of seconds, it was off the road and flipped over in the ditch. I was knocked unconscious and awoke face down in water and mud. I had been thrown from the vehicle. I remember little after that but was later told that the people who lived across the road heard the accident and came running to see if I was okay. By the time they got there, I was already walking aimlessly in the field not understanding what had transpired.

They told me that they had a difficult time getting me to tell them my name and where I lived. They called the police who were kind enough to call a tow truck and drive me home. I was completely covered in mud. The mud in my hair was drying and plastered to my face. My clothes were heavy and encased with mud. My shoes were gone.

The police got in touch with Paul, and he called my friend Ellen to help him get me out of my clothes and into a hot bath.

"Please be careful!" I was crying. I hurt all over. The slightest movement was painful and my neck was especially sore. I silently thanked God that Jason had not been with me.

Paul and Ellen, who was a nurse, assessed that nothing was broken and I assured them I just needed to rest. Ellen gave me a sleeping aid and after the two of them helped me into bed, I fell asleep.

Paul was livid and wanted to sue Ford Motor Company. He had the truck towed to the dealership we purchased it from and their mechanics claimed that driver error had caused my crash. Paul knew they were wrong. After my accident, he researched the make and model of our truck and discovered there had been a problem with the steering mechanism seizing. Had we taken it elsewhere we might have received a completely different analysis. Insurance did cover the damage, and we didn't have the means to fight a large corporation. We reluctantly had to let it go.

My training in nutrition served me well, and I knew what I needed in order to recover quickly. My healing process was quick and I was so glad to be alive. I purchased several large nursery plants for our home as I wanted to be surrounded by new life.

I became obsessed with trying new recipes, baking succulent

goodies, and keeping an immaculate home. Nothing out of place, everything as perfect as possible – these were my daily goals. I think I was trying to make up for all the past mistakes and poor decisions by doing the best I could in my new role as full-time homemaker.

Less than a month after my dad died we received a phone call that shook our world once again. Paul answered the phone and I did not know who was on the other end of the line, but I could tell it was not good news. Paul slumped into the closest chair and I watched his face drop. I wanted to know what was going on and kept whispering to him, "Who is it? What's wrong?"

He held up his hand in a gesture to silence me, and I became more frightened. When he finally hung up the phone, he just stared at me for a brief moment that seemed like forever.

"There's been an accident, Laura was killed!" Laura was his brother's wife.

"What? How?"

"She had just spoken at a woman's meeting and was on her way to pick up her little girl from daycare." He was crying slightly as he continued. "No one knows how it happened. It was a single car accident on a highway off-ramp. She was killed on impact."

Laura was young, vibrant and had three young children. Paul's brother, Al, the head of a large missionary organization, was in England on a speaking tour when he got the phone call about his wife.

It was just a couple weeks later that Paul's mother called again. She was crying. She had just received a phone call from one of her seven sisters. Four of them were traveling on a highway in Alberta and when they came to a crest of a hill, a police car was stopped in the middle of the lane without any warning lights. They swerved to miss him and hit a car head on. Three of them were killed instantly.

I was still grieving my father's death in the middle of all this tragedy. It was all so surreal -- like a nightmare I knew I would wake up from to find our family well. I didn't. I missed my dad so much. How I wished he had been here to help me through this grief. He wasn't. If only he had been here, it would have been easier. We each had to grieve in our own way and deal with it as well as we could. Sharing our good memories helped with the healing process.

Paul's mom came for her annual visit. It must have been a great relief for her to see us living a normal life. During her stay, she planted the idea of me starting a business selling my desserts, to earn an income from my home. She helped me decide which of my desserts would sell well in restaurants. We made lists of ingredients and the costs involved, and I made up a menu of about 20 desserts.

I had no idea how the restaurant owners would respond – either they would love my menu or not give me the time of day. I convinced myself that my presentation was irresistible and maintained that attitude as I approached my first prospective client. As I approached The Cannery, my stomach was queasy and my palms started to sweat. I was excited at the potential and yet feared rejection.

I approached the hostess. "May I speak to the manager please?"

She asked "Why?" and I didn't know what to say. I was concerned that if I told her the truth, she would turn me away.

"I have a proposition for him and would appreciate just a few minutes of his time." There, I thought, that was short, to the point and didn't really give out any information.

"Wait here." I waited about ten minutes which gave me time to make some observations. It was a very busy kitchen in a large restaurant. I noticed the decadent desserts in the cooler and felt intimidated but told myself that looking beautiful had nothing to do with down-home taste. I hated plastic tasting desserts, and I had confidence my list would be a winner.

The manager finally appeared. He was younger than I expected and seemed slightly agitated. I knew I could not waste his time.

"Thank you for seeing me. I bake the greatest homemade desserts that would complement your menu. I would appreciate it if you would permit me to discuss them with you." I handed him my menu.

Without even a glance at the list he asked, "Can you make a chocolate mousse cake?"

"Absolutely, I make one of the best!" I had no idea what a chocolate mousse cake was but did not want to miss this opportunity.

"Make me one and bring it in for me to try, then we'll talk." I left excited and terrified with no clue where to start. Mother, my greatest fan, was waiting for me at home. She was convinced I would sell them my entire menu.

I went to the library and looked up every chocolate mousse cake recipe I could find. That weekend, Paul helped me make 24 chocolate mousse cakes – all different yet very much the same. I didn't like any one of them. It seemed hopeless until I had a brainwave. I decided to make a cake that appealed to my taste instead of what I thought the restaurant would like. We couldn't believe the fabulous result. It was creamy; and smooth as velvet. I was ready to go back.

Walking into the restaurant with cake in hand, I sauntered past the patrons as they ogled the cake and asked if it was on the menu.

"Is Mark busy? I have a cake to deliver." I was led to the kitchen and set my prizewinner down. He stuck his finger in the cake.

"This is the best chocolate mousse cake I have ever tasted – whose recipe is it?"

"It's mine." I said proudly. "And if you give me enough orders, I will make them exclusively for you."

"Bring me three this week and ten for the weekend."

I could hardly believe my ears. Just like that I was in business. As I was leaving he added, "Oh, and bring me a couple of your other creations as well. We'll try them on the menu this weekend." He was willing to trust me with making this choice for him, yet he still had not looked at my menu.

My business took off faster than I could have ever dreamed. I averaged over 70 desserts weekly to this restaurant alone. I approached other restaurants and each one wanted my desserts. I featured different ones at each venue along with a signature creation that was theirs to advertise exclusively, like a strawberry margarita pie for the Mexican restaurant or a blitz torte for the German restaurant. I was in my element. I hired help but the workload was still overwhelming, so Paul decided to work with me three days each weekend.

We made a great team and were enjoying our new venture. I did the ordering and shopping while he did the prep. While I made desserts, he did the cleanup. We were doing all this out of my one oven, one dishwasher, and small, one-sink kitchen. It was fun and Jason was with us playing and "helping" when he could.

Thanks to our additional income, we were able to make complete restitution to our accusers, as promised, for the $12,000 they had invested in our jewelry business. We also paid off all the debts incurred by not following through with opening the jewelry store. I knew we would never receive any kind of apology, but I hoped we would receive some form of thank you. We never did.

Paul had applied for and received a full pardon from the Government of Canada. We had been waiting patiently for this so we could finalize his immigration into the U. S., where we were living. For the ten years we lived there, he had to reapply for a new visa every six months. Once we secured the full pardon, we applied for permanent status. We expected it to be just a matter of paperwork and time.

It was a long drawn-out process with the usual hoops to jump through and the endless red tape and forms. We were confident we would soon be able to live legally in our home without any more visas.

We were very proud of our garden with 80 plus rosebushes and various other flowering bushes but it took a lot of work. As busy as we were with the dessert business on weekends, we had finished early one Saturday and were working outside. It was spring time and the air was fresh but the gardens needed tending. Paul was mowing the lawn and I was weeding the garden. A car we didn't recognize pulled into the driveway.

I have often wished I had the sense that dogs do, to smell trouble or fear or other negative emotions. Our Sheltie sensed something we did not and barked loudly. I welcomed the caller and put Perky in the house.

"Sorry about that, may I help you?"

Mr. Business Suit was straight from central casting with his Navy blue wrinkled blazer that fit poorly, a white shirt with wrinkled collar, and striped tie. He presented me with his business card and showed me his credentials. "Are you Carol Graham?" I immediately realized he had come regarding Paul's immigration, and I was embarrassed about the way I looked. I was covered in dirt from kneeling in the garden, my hair unkempt and no make-up, of course.

"I would like to interview you regarding Mr. Graham's immigration application." No warning, no appointment, nothing. He just showed up.

The interview went amazingly well. He spent about two hours asking me about our marriage, our financial position, our future hopes. I felt more confident answering each question and knew the approval would be forthcoming. So it was with this confidence we opened the letter from the United States Immigration and Naturalization Service some months later.

Dear Mr. Graham, it began, we regret. That's all I remember reading. We regret. I felt too weak to stand and fell onto my knees and began to cry. Another disappointment. Another setback. Now what were we going to do?

The letter continued to inform us that permanent residency status could not be granted because moving back to Canada would not cause severe financial hardship for Paul. He was married to a U. S. citizen, owned a home in the U. S., had an American born child and I had a thriving business in the community. Apparently this was not adequate, in their estimation, to cause a severe enough financial hardship for us if we moved to Canada. Paul's temporary visa was revoked the next day. Our unrecognized financial hardship was about to begin.

We launched our appeal. The process was almost as long as the original one. Paperwork and interviews. Such a waste of time and money. I wondered if they had even read the original documents. Who sat at a desk, after a bad day, and decided to turn our world upside down? We worked hard. We contributed to the community. It was completely unjust.

We received a letter in the mail for a final review with the Appellate Board regarding Paul's immigration. I went with great anticipation that our current situation was about to change for the better and that Paul would be able to live at home, once again.

I cried, I begged, I reasoned. The gavel was lowered. The answer was a resounding "NO." To make matters worse, Paul was not allowed to enter the U. S. ever again because he had a criminal record. Apparently, the pardon he had received from the Government of Canada had no bearing on the United States Immigration decision.

The first order of business was to put our house on the market. It saddened me deeply as I walked through the garden where we had laughed at the sight of our Doberman standing on her hind legs eating plums off the tree in the backyard. There was the small pond that Jason loved to play around. It was quiet and serene. The rose garden was so beautiful and our dogs were free to run. I would watch from the house while Jason played in the front yard and our Sheltie kept an eye on him at the end of the driveway. If Jason got too close to the road, she would literally grab him by his pants and shepherd him back home. It was a little bit of country very close to the city and I didn't want to move.

"I really only see one option here" Paul told me, "and that is for me to live in my office."

"That is absurd! Where would you sleep? There's no shower. Don't be ridiculous!"

"Do you have a better idea? We can't afford two households."

The same anger and sorrow I had worked through when he went to jail began to overtake me.

"Maybe the house will sell quickly, and we will be able to live together again soon." I tried to sound optimistic but it was the early 1980s and the real estate market was in a crisis.

Somehow he convinced me. I packed up a few things for him to take to the office and agreed to bring his food and fresh clothes every evening. I continued my dessert business and each day I would also make a nice meal, pack it and Jason into the car and drive to Canada to have dinner with Paul.

"Where are you headed?" The border patrol would ask me.

"Taking my husband his dinner."

"So, I guess you will be leaving it in Canada?"

It became a standard joke with the border guards, and they were very kind about it. Most of them were sympathetic but there was nothing they could do to help me.

Paul made a bed out of a sleeping bag on the floor in the spare room of his office and sometimes we would stay with him for the night. Jason loved the adventure of camping out with Daddy. I did not share that feeling.

We decided that if we were to have any kind of family life, Paul had to find a way to come home. There was a road, which circled Point Roberts, where The United States of America was on one side and Canada on the other. The unique border crossing was not patrolled and so lax that it was actually possible to tend a Canadian garden, which had spread itself onto U. S. soil. On the east side of Point Roberts is the beach of Boundary Bay and even the U. S. border patrol can't put a fence in an ocean.

People walked freely back and forth. All summer long, people on the beach would spend half their time in Canada and half in the U. S. They were not supposed to, but it was totally open so they weren't too concerned about getting caught. We knew that it was a much greater risk for us because if Paul got caught coming across the border it would be a federal offense.

On weekends, we decided we would take that risk and devised many different schemes to get Paul across the border. Sometimes he cut through someone's yard after dark. Sometimes he walked on the beach, and I picked him up at different spots. Sometimes he crept through a wooded area and jumped into the car as I drove by. It was always nerve racking and scary. I never wanted to take for granted that we would not be caught. We were well aware of the danger and the adrenalin was always pumping when we took this risk. There was no enjoyment to this game of cat and mouse, but we saw no other choice and Jason was so happy to see Daddy jump into the backseat.

Home was about a mile from the border. Once we got there, we spent the weekend with the drapes drawn, and did not answer the door or the telephone. Jason was young enough that he didn't ask any questions and was just thrilled to have his daddy home.

On our weekends together, Paul helped me with the desserts and spent as much time with Jason as possible. He was a great dad who got down on the floor with him to play with Lego and trucks and games. We enjoyed having our meals together at a table instead of an office desk.

It was stressful though. If the phone rang, we jumped. When a car drove by, we held our breath. It was a constant concern, but we were happy to be together.

"Hi honey, I have a surprise for you." Paul called to tell me just before coming home one weekend. Instantly, I thought of several things that would make the weekend special but was not prepared for what he said next.

"I made a trade today for a Moluccan Cockatoo and have to bring him home for the weekend." I didn't have a clue what that was but figured it was a bird.

"If we like him, we can keep him; but if he doesn't work out, I will find a buyer for him." Fair enough, I thought, and hoped it would be a fun playmate for Jason.

When we picked him up, he was carrying a large cage with a towel draped over it. He was also carrying a large perch, taller than himself.

"How big IS this bird?" I asked.

"I'll show you when we get home." He was grinning ear to ear and excitedly telling Jason about this beautiful white bird with orange feathers on the top of his head.

"If you like him, you can keep him." I was upset he hadn't discussed this with me. I had owned birds as a young girl, and they always left big messes to clean up. I was already dreading the addition of this chore to my busy days.

"Don't get too excited, honey," I told Jason. "Let's see what he is like first."

"Hello, my name is Echo! Hello, my name is Echo! HELLO, my name is ECHO!" That is the only thing he could say and he repeated it constantly. He got louder if we didn't pay attention to him.

"You won't believe what happened on my way to meet you," Paul told us. "I could hear someone approaching so I tried to act nonchalant about carrying a bird through the woods. A guy walked past me with his German shepherd from the U. S. side of the border. The bird kept yelling 'HELL-O MY NAME IS ECHO!' The dog barked which made me nervous, but I just kept walking knowing that neither one of us was supposed to be there. The other guy was probably as nervous as me."

It was quite funny when Paul told us this story but the humor quickly wore thin when the bird would not shut up – ever. All night long, he squawked. During the day, he talked and screeched. It was not a melodious bird song but rather a high-pitched, ear-popping squeal. With this noise came an attitude. He liked no one. He was vicious and didn't think twice about biting the hand that fed him.

We weren't sure if Echo was always like that or just very unhappy to be with us. I approached his perch with oven mitts on my hands which only made him go for my face or arm. Then he would turn on himself and start pulling out his feathers.

When his bites drew blood and we had to keep putting cotton in our ears to stifle the noise, we decided the best place for Echo was in the back yard shed. We were terrified to think what he might do to Jason if we didn't get rid of him. On Monday morning, we convinced a pet shop to take him and they absolutely loved the adorable, sweet creature. He was the only pet I have never missed.

Each week we counted the days until Paul would come home again. Yet, the fear of the risk involved was overwhelming and constantly in our thoughts.

I vacillated between dwelling on it and trying not to think about it. Paul would plan a different spot to cross each week to keep us from becoming complacent. We wanted to maintain an edge and stay on the alert.

Our weekends meant not leaving the house or socializing at all. It was difficult, but we were thankful to spend the time together. We watched movies, played games and played with Jason and the dogs in the backyard. Always on the alert, always looking around us, always on edge. When we heard a car approaching Paul would run and hide in a closet or the shed outside. We had many false alarms, but couldn't take any chances.

I kept very busy with my dessert business and was so thankful for the full-time income. Then one day I received a surprise phone call asking me to meet with the owner of a new restaurant that was being built.

"Carol, I have heard about your dessert business and its success and have a proposition for you. Would you be able to meet me at the job site of the club I am building?"

I was surprised and flattered as she continued. "It is going to have a seating capacity of 1,100 people, and I am planning on bringing in live bands Thursdays through Sunday nights. I want it to be first rate and would like to feature your desserts, exclusively."

She continued with her sales pitch when we met on the site and explained that she would like to lease the space to me for a bistro. I would be able to serve any type of food I wanted along with my desserts. They were open from lunchtime to closing at 2 A.M. seven days a week. I would, however, be financially responsible for all the equipment that was needed to set up the bistro. It all sounded very exciting but would depend on what Paul thought of the proposal. He agreed it was a great idea, and it would give me a proper kitchen to work out of instead of my home.

We sought the advice of a friend of ours who was a chef and he helped with a menu plan and buying the equipment we needed. I was able to obtain a bank loan for $20,000 and we were in business.

My other restaurant clients were very disappointed I had decided to go this route, as it meant I would not be making desserts for them, but were also pleased for this opportunity for me.

Opening day was fast approaching and the whole town was talking about the new restaurant and how much business it would bring to the Point. When I overheard people talking about it, I invited them to see me at the Bistro for a free dessert. I was both proud and excited, looking forward to opening day. We featured live bands in a huge facility but our big drawing card was that alcohol was served on Sundays, which was prohibited in Canada. Of course this would bring a lot of business into my adjoining bistro.

That first day we served food to over 3,300 people. We ran out of almost everything by midnight and scratched together whatever we could until closing I had never seen anything like it. I punched in the numbers on the register, took the cash, and moved on to the next person all day long. The line-up was so fast and so busy that most of the time I didn't even look up. It was both exhausting and exhilarating. It was also dreamlike. If this was a taste of what was going to happen every weekend, we would soon be able to finance another residence for Paul until our home sold.

We realized our opening day numbers couldn't possibly continue to be that large; but even if they dropped to half, we would be laughing. I just couldn't believe this opportunity had come my way.

I did as much baking as I could at home in order to spend time with Jason. When I was working at the bistro, he would stay at my friend's home. She ran a daycare and Jason loved being there with the other children. One day I was making cookies; and I noticed that as I rolled them out and placed them on the cookie sheets, the numbers were decreasing instead of increasing. Then I caught my precious little boy playing catch with the dog. The dog was eating my profits. I had to stop and have a good laugh and put it all into perspective. I remembered my first priority was to my family and realized I would have to hire help to keep those priorities in order.

Our second weekend was almost as big as our first. The numbers were still over 2,000 and the future looked increasingly promising. No one could have predicted what happened next, not even the owner of the restaurant who had invested several million dollars.

That Friday's headlines in the Vancouver Sun announced, "ALCOHOL NOW SERVED ON SUNDAYS." The following weekend, instead of having hoards of people waiting in line at the door, we only had 100 in total in our monstrosity of a restaurant. No amount of advertising or specials could change it in the weeks to follow. Canadians would stay in Canada for their dining entertainment on Sundays. We walked away after a few months with a large debt. Shortly, thereafter, the beautiful establishment was boarded up and it never reopened.

Discouragement, confusion, bewilderment, and embarrassment -- I felt it all. Why was life such a struggle? I often wondered where God was and why everything seemed to be going wrong, but never lost faith that there were better days ahead. I believed God cared very much for me and someday we would look back at everything that happened as stepping-stones to a better life. And then it happened.

Chapter Eight

Saturday – remember the one that started out like all other Saturdays. Jason and I picked Paul up at the airport. We arrived home to plainclothes officers rapping at our front door and Paul fleeing through the back. This Saturday started an endless chain of events.

My sharpest memories were shrouded in darkness. No amount of faith or hope in the future could change the past. It haunted us wherever we went and colored whatever decisions we made. It was as if I woke up one day and realized this was not the life I set out to have when I graduated from high school with dreams of a comfortable future. I wanted to start over, to reset my life. But the only thing I could do was to put one foot in front of the other and continue, hoping this cloud had a silver lining.

I walked home from the border office chilled to the bone and terrified. My thoughts raced with questions. Where was Paul? It had been four hours since I last saw him. Did he try calling me when I was in the border office? Who can I call? Where should I go? An officer had taken Jason to his daycare; should I pick him up?

I was so blessed to have Jason at Pat's Day Care. Pat came into my life when Jason was only fifteen months old. Jason was accepted at his young age because he was so bright and alert. Normally, she did not accept children less than eighteen months of age. Pat was a warm, gentle, yet firm teacher who taught me a great deal about child rearing. You could walk into her daycare at any time and it would be structured. The children were happy and learning life skills as well. She ran it like a large family where all members, regardless of age, participated in chores and helping one another. It was like a second home for Jason, and I could rest assured that he would always be safe and cared for even if I had to leave him overnight.

I paced back and forth in our hallway. My stomach ached. My head hurt. My heart was dense. Fear of the unknown left me weak and exhausted. My hands were trembling. I stared at the phone hoping it would ring and terrified it wouldn't.

When it did ring, I jumped. I didn't know if I should answer it. I didn't want anyone to know what was going on but what if Paul was calling. I had to answer it.

It wasn't Paul. It was the mechanic's wife, Debbie. I liked her and we had coffee together a few times while I was waiting for my car to be repaired, but I did not want to chat right now.

"Hi Carol."

"Hi Debbie." I said with a question in my voice.

"I was wondering if you could come over for a coffee and tell me about Shaklee."

I thought, is this woman nuts, calling me late on Saturday evening? I tried to remain calm when answering her.

"I am really kinda busy. Could we make it another time?"

"Carol, I really need you to come over immediately. I need to order some vitamins and it can't wait." There was urgency in her voice, and I realized her call had nothing to do with vitamins. I was curious, excited, and terrified.

"I'll be right there." I managed to answer.

I grabbed a sweater, threw some water on my tear-stained face and got into my car. I could not keep my hand steady enough to get the key in the ignition. Nausea swept over me. I bit down on my tongue to gain some composure and backed out of the driveway

Debbie and Jack lived about a mile down the road, next door to their auto repair shop. I knocked and Debbie opened the door.

I almost collapsed and had to steady myself against the door frame. There was Paul sitting at the kitchen table having a cup of coffee. His face was ashen. His whole body was trembling and he had trouble holding the cup.

He stood up and held me in his arms while I cried. "What are you doing here? Is this safe? What are we going to do?"

He began to explain, "I walked through the woods until I got to the main road. Jack's place was right across the street, and I waited until the coast was clear and then ran across."

He knew what I was going to ask next. "I had to tell them what happened. It was only fair and I can't keep them in harm's way any longer. You have got to get me across the border."

"And just how do you expect me to do that?" The thought made a shudder with a chill running up my spine.

Debbie looked uncomfortable and Jack seemed agitated. I

didn't blame either one of them and felt terrible for putting them in this situation.

I began to cry, "Thank you both so much for doing this for us. Your kindness goes far beyond anything I could have imagined. I don't know how we will ever be able to thank you." My words seemed empty but had to be said.

The three of them had formed a plan. "Debbie is going to loan you her car, and I will be in the trunk. I'm going to hold the trunk door slightly open and when we get to the beach area, tap your brakes three times and I'll jump out."

I was sure there was no way we could pull this off. The borders were being watched. "We could both end up in jail."

"I know exactly what you are thinking Babe, but we have no choice."

The tears came easy now, as I knew he was right. I was exhausted and my nervousness didn't allow me to think lucidly.

Jason was still at the daycare and it was quite late. I knew that Pat would have fed him and put him to bed. I realized she had no idea what was going on, but I took some comfort in also knowing she would never inquire.

I quickly went home and got a jacket, shoes and socks for Paul. When he ran out the back door that morning, he was in his stocking feet and had since spent several hours in the wet snow. I knew he would have preferred a warm bath but that was out of the question.

When I walked into our home, I could smell the beef roast. It was still in the slow cooker. I unplugged it and wondered whether

Paul would ever be home again. I realized then that part of my nausea was due to hunger but there wasn't any time. The baby within me was draining me even more, but I was still unaware of her existence.

I grabbed what I needed and headed back to the mechanic's. I drove slowly, watching for any car lights, not knowing what I would do if I spotted another car. Fortunately, there were none.

Jack had opened his shop door and I drove inside. I ran into their house and gave Paul the change of clothes for his long trek across the beach and then a couple of miles further to his office.

Debbie gave me her car keys and said "Good luck, you'll need it!" That wasn't very reassuring but we had come this far and couldn't think of any other solution.

After Paul was in the trunk, I jumped in the car and headed in the opposite direction of the border. I went the long away around the Point taking side roads and weaving my way back to the border by Boundary Bay beach. It was pitch dark with no streetlights. Jack had removed the trunk light, and I drove slowly enough hoping I would not alert anyone.

I thanked God for the clouds and the absence of moonlight. As I approached the beach, I noticed that even the few houses on the beach were dark. It was February and most of them were summer cottages that were not used this time of year.

I tapped the brake three times and stopped for only a moment. My windows were closed, and I didn't even hear him jump out but I felt the car shift and knew he was gone.

I wanted to circle the area to be sure he made it across the border but didn't risk it. In my mind the border guards were on surveillance with guns drawn. I breathed a prayer begging God to protect both of us and was crying so hard I could barely see well enough to drive.

I knew Pat would be asleep and I would not need to call her. I just wanted to go home, lock the door, have a bath, and pretend this never happened.

I was still shaking when I put the key in the front door. What would I do if someone was there watching me and ask me where my car was? What would I say?

"Just get the key in the door and unlock it. Close it behind you, lock it and stay calm." I told myself. Easier said than done.

Where is Paul now? Did he make it across? Did they catch him? Is he back in jail?

A bath was out of the question until I knew what was going on. It was a full hour later when the call came.

"Hi Babe."

"Are you all right?" I realized quickly I had to speak in code. "What did you do tonight?"

"I'm really tired and just want to go to bed. Just calling to say good-night. I'll see you tomorrow."

Short and sweet – but those words were right up there with "You have a healthy baby boy." They gave me the peace I needed.

It felt like the story of my entire day was written on my face for everyone to read. I was the only criminal in the world and everyone was watching me, waiting for me to make a stupid mistake. I knew this was not the end of it.

I bathed and tried to watch some TV to take my mind off the

situation. Sleep was out of the question. I cried until I didn't think I could produce any more tears. I was glad the next day would be Sunday. We could spend the day together and decide our next move.

Early Sunday morning I called Pat to tell her I was on my way to get Jason. As expected, she never asked any questions and I did not offer any explanations.

"We are going to go find Daddy and spend the day with him," was my explanation to Jason. It was enough information for him. He was just excited to see his Dad.

I tried to remain totally calm when I pulled up to the border station. I knew there would be an alert out regarding yesterday's events. The guard asked me the usual questions as he stared deeply into my eyes.

"Where you going?" he asked.

"To Tsawwassen." I answered and smiled.

"Dropping anything off in Canada?" I felt like saying that I already did last night and that made me smile inside.

"No, just visiting someone there."

We were waved through. It was easy this time, but I thought they were bound to treat me differently in the future.

Paul looked pretty shaken. I supposed he had not slept well. How could he have?

"What will they do if they figure out what we did?" I asked with tears in my eyes. "What if Jack and Debbie say something?"

"They won't say anything. They have no reason to. There is no way they can prove what we did so stop worrying about it." His words were reassuring.

We spent the day talking about what we should do next. Paul said that he would try to find a place for us to live in Canada, and we would be together soon. He said that once we were settled in Canada this would all be behind us, and we could live without feeling as though we were under surveillance.

I agreed that it would be an extreme relief and was looking forward to it. Days turned into weeks, and I continued to bring dinners to Paul, take his laundry home, run my dessert business, and deal with creditors wanting to be paid for my purchases for the bistro. I had my moments of tears, but I kept my fears from Paul and Jason.

Living in a small town, I knew that I was the subject of whispers and innuendos. Several of the border guards lived on the Point, and I was certain they would be telling their friends what had happened. News was bound to travel fast so I held my head up high and pretended nothing had happened. I told no one.

It was the middle of March, and I was having a lot of abdominal pain. I shared this with a friend and her instant response was "Have you missed your period?"

"I've never been regular so I have no idea."

"Well, have you been emotional lately?"

I admitted I had but could not tell her why.

"Girl, you are pregnant!"

"PREGNANT? No way." I wanted to cry and to laugh at the same time.

She continued, "Of course you are. You have all the classic symptoms. When I was pregnant I could feel my womb stretching and it wasn't pleasant. I was so emotional that I would cry at anything."

Could she be right? It had been 14 years since I stood in front of that doctor who shook his finger at me when I refused to have a hysterectomy and said "Then, lady, go home, suffer and die!"

I made an appointment. Paul was as excited as I was and wanted to be with me at the doctor's office. He was surprised but pleased that I chose to go back to that same doctor. He knew it would bring me pleasure to rub my pregnancy in the doctor's face.

We sat in the waiting room for only 20 minutes but it seemed like hours. We both hoped I was pregnant but didn't want to get too excited prematurely.

"If you aren't pregnant, what do you think is going on?" Paul whispered.

"I have no idea. There is really no other explanation. I don't think there is anything wrong with me. My health has improved so much."

I was doing my best to remain composed. Inside, my stomach was doing flip-flops. What if I am pregnant? Will we live together before the baby is born? How am I going to be able to keep up my pace?

"Carol." The nurse called me into the treatment room.

"Why are you here?" She asked.

"I need a physical. I haven't had one for a while."

She asked me to put on a gown and leave a urine sample in the adjoining bathroom. I was ready in a few minutes but still very jittery.

"Hello, Carol. It has been a while since I have seen you. Why did you decide to come now?" I couldn't believe how old the doctor looked. He seemed to have aged much more than 14 years.

"I haven't had a physical for a long time and figured I should." I began to imagine what he would say if I were actually pregnant. And what would I say?

He examined me and tried to make small talk. I was not interested. My thoughts were focused and I could hardly contain myself. I wanted to blurt out "I'm pregnant, you idiot!"

He left the room and said he would return shortly when he got the lab results from my urine sample. It was 1:12 P.M. I wondered how long a few minutes would be as I stared at the clock and watched it move ever so slowly. One minute, then two. Five minutes went by.

"I'm not pregnant." I thought to myself. "If I were, I would have known by now." I almost started to cry and wondered what I would say to him if I was wrong. I hadn't thought about that.

Ten minutes, then fifteen. "He'll be right with you." The nurse popped her head in the room to tell me.

It was a full half hour when the doctor walked back in. If I thought he looked old before, he had visibly aged in those last 30 minutes.

"Carol, I am very sorry to inform you, but you are very pregnant." His head was down as if he were ashamed.

I stood up. "Yes, doctor, I...am...sure.... you... are... very... sorry... to.... inform... me. You obviously remember the words you spoke to me the last time I was here. What do you have to say about that?"

I was not prepared in any way for the next words that came out of his mouth. Trying to gain his composure and his rightful position, he stood up and whispered a shout, "Who is the father?" He threw the words at me, the same way he had all those years ago.

I thought maybe, just maybe, he would apologize to me or even be happy for me. I never expected him to be angry.

He must have remembered, or read it in my file, that Paul was sterile. I knew he was no longer sterile because the same God who opened my womb corrected his sperm. God had promised us children and this was indeed a miracle. Paul had received a report some months earlier of healthy sperm. There was no way I was going to waste my breath by telling the doctor. Clearly, he wanted to intimidate me with the little dirty secret he thought he had. I clenched my hands to keep myself from punching him in his sleazy little mouth. I could have said so many things just then, but I was too elated with the news. I wanted out of his awful room that reeked of pharmaceuticals. I made a waving gesture with my hands indicating I wanted to get dressed. He left and I never saw him again.

I met Paul in the waiting area with a huge smile on my face. When he saw me, I thought he was going to cry. I didn't have to say a word. We hugged.

We went straight to the Canadian Passport office in downtown Vancouver. Paul needed to renew his passport and when we walked in, I am sure we were glowing. The room smacked of government boredom, with no color or personality. One glance around the crowded office made us feel like strangers in our own land. Most of the people were of foreign descent and very few were speaking English.

Without any warning, my reserved, conservative husband

stood up on a chair, cupped his hands around his mouth, and made a trumpet-like announcement to the hundred plus people in the room.

"MY.....WIFE.....IS   GOING.........TO........HAVE.........A BABY!"

He was grinning like a little kid who had just performed an act that made him very proud of himself. I think he frightened most of the people there, as they did not understand what he was doing or saying. I was shocked, surprised and pleased. I wanted to laugh and cry. The news genuinely hit me – I was going to have a baby.

It was March 1986 and Paul felt an urgency to go to China. We talked about it. He wasn't sure why, but the more he thought about it, the more he felt compelled to go. He had never been to China before, he knew no one there, and we really didn't have the funds. But he felt so strongly about it that we had to make plans.

"Honey, if you feel that you must go, then, you must go. We will find a way to work it out." I know that was a relief for him, and we proceeded to make plans.

"Are you sure you are comfortable with this? I won't be gone long, and I know it will give me a chance to put things into perspective as well. I have made so many mistakes in my life that have caused us such grief. Going away might be the therapy I need to plan our future."

I assured him that I would be fine. I was feeling good, and I knew it would be a good break for him. Paul's Dad had been living right next door for a few years and would be able to help me if needed.

We got enough money together for a one-way ticket. We both felt it was important for him to go as quickly as possible. I assured

Paul that I would be able to make enough to wire the return fare to him in a week or so. He left for China on a one-way ticket and $140 cash in his pocket.

This first trip he was gone about four weeks. I worked steady in my dessert business and was able to get the money together and wire it to him for his return.

When Jason and I picked him up at the airport, Paul was incredibly happy. It was so good to see him like that. We were anxious to hear about his venture and why he had felt it was so important to go there.

"When I landed in Hong Kong I had no idea where I was to go or what I was to do. The city is like one big open market, and I began to check out the street vendors. You can buy anything, absolutely anything on the street and the prices are pennies compared to what they are here."

"Wish I could have gone shopping with you!" I dreamed.

"I found a guest house to stay overnight in Kowloon and the next morning I found a map of China posted on a big board on the street. Guilan, a city in South Central China, stood out and seemed to be beckoning me. I felt it so strongly that I decided to go there."

I was fascinated as he continued. We had stopped for some dinner and realized that people in the restaurant were overhearing and enjoying our conversation. It made me smile inside.

"I asked the owner of the guest house the cheapest way to get to China. He spoke fluent English and told me to take the two-hour train ride to the border and then walk through Customs to get across. I was sitting at the train station looking at a map when a man approached me and asked me where I was going. He said he was traveling in the same direction and would get me onto the right train. He sat in another car but kept coming back to my car to check up on me. When we got off the train, I was so glad to have his help. I found myself surrounded by thousands of people and didn't have a clue where to go. It was wall-to-wall people. He said he wanted to take me to dinner, which he paid for, and then booked me into a hotel."

"Incredible!"

"The next morning when I got up he had already gone down to the ferry dock and purchased my ticket, which he would not take any money for, and paid the hotel bill as well as the taxi to the ferry."

"Unbelievable – from a total stranger!"

"I tried to give him money but he just wouldn't hear of it! It was as if I was insulting him by offering. We parted and it felt like I was leaving a good friend."

I could tell Paul was reliving the trip and enjoyed every minute telling me about it. Jason sat unusually still; hanging on to his daddy's every word.

"From there I took a two-day boat trip up the Yellow River to Wozhou, stayed overnight and then took a bus to Guilan."

"Isn't that where you were headed in the first place? Seems like such a long way to get there!"

"Yes, but what a trip. It was a brand new Mercedes bus and it was packed. The driver didn't know how to work the air conditioner and it was about 95 degrees outside and very humid. The roads are very curvy and the driver was going very fast. People started to throw up and the more they did, the more other people did! I was keeping my eyes closed and using everything in me to hold down my food. By the time we stopped, all the windows on both sides of the bus looked like a sheet of white rice."

I laughed, but I felt like throwing up just hearing about it.

"I got off the bus in Guilin, booked myself into a hotel and went for a walk. I was standing on a bridge when I noticed a floating restaurant. I felt compelled to go down to it. There I was dead center in China, and I could not believe what I saw. Inside the restaurant was a large banner. In English, in very bold letters, it said, 'For God so loved the world that He gave His only begotten Son that whosoever believes on Him, shall not perish but have eternal life.'" (John 3:16)

"I asked to see the restaurant owner, and a man who spoke fluent English came to my table. I asked him what the banner meant, and he told me about God and His love. I told him I was a Christian as well and we formed an instant bond. I stayed there several days; and he told me that if I wanted to come back and go on a speaking tour in China, he would be able to get me into universities and schools, and he would interpret for me. John supplied my meals, took me sight-seeing on his motorcycle and offered me a place to stay when I came back."

"I wanted to see more of this amazing country and decided to go to Shanghai. I had to take a bus to Wuhan and then another ferry down the Yangtze River to get there. When I got on the ferry, I checked out the dining room and started taking a video of it. The chef watched me do that and got very excited. He thought he was about to become a movie star. It was very humorous, and I took lots of pictures of him and the kitchen. That night when I went to the dining room for dinner it was packed. He saw me and went over to a table of people and made them leave so I could sit down. I was so embarrassed and certainly could not understand what he told the people, but he made me sit and eat. He did this for three days straight and never let me pay for any food!"

"When we parted I felt I was leaving another good friend behind, and I had to swallow hard to keep back the emotion because of his kindness."

I felt close to tears and gave Paul a hug but it still wasn't clear to me why he had gone.

"Even with all the kind-heartedness of strangers my $140 was almost gone, and I still had to get back to Hong Kong. I knew that you would have wired money for my ticket back to Canada but there was no way you could send it to me in the middle of China. I stayed in a men's dormitory that night and before I went to sleep I asked God to somehow help me to get enough money for the trip back."

"Well, you made it back, so what in the world happened?"

"When I woke up in the morning, all the men were gone and on the floor tucked into one of my shoes was enough money for my trip. It was clearly meant for me, and I will never know how it got there."

I felt both exhausted and exhilarated listening to this story. There were so many details to think about. I saw how God had taken care of him every step of the way, and I knew this was only the beginning of a new life for us.

Chapter Nine

My niece, Ashley, from Wisconsin, had just graduated from high school and wanted to visit us for a couple weeks. I was excited to have her come as Paul was planning another trip to China as soon as he could.

We were able to get the extra funds together from both my business and Paul's and he headed out on his second trip. He realized the potential of bringing back giftware to sell, and he also wanted to see John in Guilan. He was elated to be going back after only two months and glad that Ashley would be with me.

Ashley arrived at the airport on the same day Paul left for China. She and I stayed up late chatting and catching up with everything that was happening in our lives. Around 3:30 in the morning I woke up desperate to go to the bathroom. I just made it in time and could not believe my eyes.

I felt something very large leave my body, and I was terrified to look in the toilet bowl. I expected it to be my baby. I thought that if I didn't look then maybe it didn't happen. But I had to look – to be certain. I thought my eyes were deceiving me. I ran to the kitchen and got a plastic container. I reached into the toilet and fished out a huge bloody object. I couldn't make out what it was and still was not sure if it was my baby. I put a lid on the container and put it into a bag so that I would not have to look at it. No one had ever told me what a miscarriage looked like, but I guessed it was like this.

Everything inside of me cried out in terror but somehow I felt a peace in the middle of that moment. When I picked up the phone to call the hospital, the line was dead. This could not be happening, I thought. There hadn't been a storm and I had paid the bill, so why wasn't the phone working? Still trying to remain calm, I gently woke Ashley and without offering an explanation that might alarm her, I told her I was going over to my friends' to use the phone as ours was not working. She was sleepy enough that she just said "okay" and rolled over.

I drove the mile to my friends and tapped on her bedroom window. She immediately realized the seriousness of my visit and invited me in. I explained what happened and asked to use her phone to call the clinic.

"I am four months pregnant," I explained to the receptionist, "and I just passed a large mass. I have kept it in a jar and need to see a doctor as quickly as possible."

"Thank you for keeping the mass as it will be much easier for the doctor to determine what is going on. Unfortunately, you won't be able to see anyone until the clinic opens at eight." She was the answering service and maybe didn't realize my urgency as I sounded so calm.

In my heart, I knew everything was going to be all right but still struggled with the feeling that something was terribly wrong. It was a teeter-totter of emotions. I knew that getting upset was not going to help anyone or change anything. All I could do was wait the four hours before going to the clinic.

I drove back home and tried to sleep – impossibility. Now my mind was racing. I still felt life inside of me and could not understand. Maybe I passed a twin. I didn't know what to think. The minutes ticked by as I stared at the clock. I tried to keep positive and prayed that God would protect my baby and me.

Finally it was seven o'clock and Jason woke up. "Good morning, precious. Guess what? You get to stay at home with Ashley while mommy goes to see the doctor. Can you show her where everything is to make your breakfast?"

"Yup!" He beamed with pride as he assumed the role of helper.

I didn't want to alarm Ashley so said nothing to make her question why I didn't tell her about the doctor's appointment the night before.

When I walked into the clinic and told the nurse what happened she grabbed a wheel chair and said, "Sit there." Within seconds a nurse brought out a gurney and two others helped me onto it. I was wheeled into an examination room and a doctor arrived almost immediately.

"What exactly happened Ms. Graham?" I explained what happened that morning and tried not to cry.

"Before I examine you I need to explain something to you.

Thank you for bringing in the mass you passed because we need to send it to Pathology to see what it is. It is NOT a baby so don't be concerned about that. However, there is a very serious problem here. Would you be able to call your husband and have him come down?"

"Sorry, that isn't possible. He is flying to China as we speak and not reachable."

As she was talking to me, two nurses were wheeling me into another room to have an ultrasound.

"Very well then. Here's the thing. I don't know what it is that you passed and at this point it does not matter. What does matter is that we will need to prep you for an emergency C section. You are going to have your baby today."

"Excuse me, did I hear you correctly? You are going to take my baby out?"

"Here is the problem, Ms. Graham. You have total placenta praevia. That means that the placenta is totally covering the cervix and in order for this mass to come out, it had to pass over the placenta and contaminate the baby. We will have to get this baby out within 24 hours or you could lose it. Bacteria will set in very quickly."

I lost all composure and started to shriek. My anger gave me the strength to be assertive. "I am not ready to have this baby. He is too small. You can't take my baby. He won't live. There has got to be another way. I don't believe you."

While I was crying, the doctor was examining me, and I could not help but notice she had a very strange look on her face. I didn't know whether to be relieved or terrified. She made a quick phone call and seconds later another doctor was examining me.

"Ms. Graham, there is no explanation to what has happened here short of a miracle. I know this is not humanly possible but your womb has sealed itself back. There is no opening. We will watch it for the next 24 hours; and if all goes well, you will be able to go home."

At this point I smiled as I knew exactly what had happened, and I also believed I knew what the mass was. God had intervened.

"Doctor, for many years I had suffered with endometriosis and I am confident that the mass was just that." I also knew, but didn't say anything, that this was a miracle in many ways.

The fact that Ashley had just arrived to visit me and was there to watch Jason was such a comfort to me.

I called Ashley and the phone was working. That will remain a mystery.

"The doctor wants to keep me in the clinic for a day just to be sure everything is fine as my ultrasound showed that something weird was happening." I thanked her profusely for being there and felt badly for not spending the day with her doing something fun.

It took three weeks for the Pathology report to come back but it was as I said – endometriosis tissue. Now I understood why I was so 'big.' I had other things growing inside me besides a baby. It was a lot easier to have it come out the way it did than go through another surgery.

The doctor allowed me to go home the next day if I promised to behave myself. I had to get a wheel chair for grocery shopping, could no longer work and was ordered to be on bed rest. She explained that if I exerted myself, the placenta could tear and the baby could come too early. I was a bit fearful but just couldn't imagine it happening.

I promised the doctor I would slow down and be careful, but I knew bed rest was out of the question. Ashley decided she would stay with me for as long as I needed her. She was enjoying her extended holiday on the coast.

I had to inform my dessert clients of my situation and was concerned how we would make it without my income. It was extremely difficult to sit around and do nothing. I would see threads on the carpet and feel the need to vacuum. It was driving me crazy so I snuck around and vacuumed or did whatever needed to be done when Ashley was not there.

The doctor wanted me to come in for weekly ultrasounds. It was wonderful watching my baby grow. The doctor informed me that there was little room left for baby as I was growing three massive tumors as well. They did not seem to think it would be a problem as long as they did not get too big, but as much as I was trying to keep things in perspective, I was worried.

Paul had come back from China more excited than I had seen him in a long time. He was planning his new venture. He had visited many giftware factories and brought in several different sample items from China. He started to take orders from local gift and jewelry stores. He was getting extremely busy, and I was so glad to have Ashley with me. She entertained Jason, cooked for us, cleaned the house, and ran errands. I was obedient, stayed off my feet and watched a lot of television. It was difficult but I kept telling myself I was doing this for my baby.

I was confident that as long as I rested and stayed off my

feet, everything would be fine. But after a few weeks, I woke with a brown stain on my panties. My confidence vanished.

There were no doctors on the Point; and if you wanted to see an American doctor, you would have to travel through Canada and cross the border into Mainland U. S. A. Under the sensitive circumstances of my condition, I knew I had to find a doctor closer to home.

I was incredibly fortunate to secure Dr. Sam Effries, head of the Gynecology Department as my doctor. Dr. Effries was highly respected by his peers and patients. He was kind, showed concern and always took the time to answer any questions. When I called his office that morning with the news, the nurse told me. "Dr. Effries wants you to come in immediately. He will fit you in whenever you get here."

Now, I definitely began to worry. I was hoping that it was just something minor and when I saw the doctor, my fears would be alleviated.

Ashley drove me into Vancouver to the hospital and after Dr. Effries examined me he said, "Carol, you are bleeding internally. This is what I was concerned might happen. You will not be able to go home. Please call your husband and have him pack a bag for you as we are admitting you."

I began to cry. "Doctor, I can't be admitted. I have a little boy and he needs me. I promise I will stay in bed and my niece will take care of me."

"You do not seem to understand the severity of this situation. It isn't just bed rest that you need; if there are further complications, you may not be able to make it to the hospital in time to save your baby."

I had more than three months left to carry this child. How was my family going to survive without me?

Yet, the other side of my brain was saying, "Now you will get the rest and care you need without having to worry about anything or anyone else. They will be fine." In that small way, I was relieved.

I called Paul to tell him to have Ashley pack a bag for me. "Please bring it to the hospital so we can discuss what to do."

Poor Ashley, I thought. It was a big responsibility to put on an eighteen-year old girl. She would have to make Paul's meals and take them to him into Canada. She would have full responsibility for Jason and the household duties such as shopping, banking, laundry, and cleaning.

I settled in quickly to life in the hospital but the days dragged by. I suffered such severe headaches that I was not able to read or even watch television. I went through a battery of tests to find out exactly what was causing my problems. An ultrasound was scheduled twice a month, and I was hooked up to a fetal monitor daily. Every time the nurses put on the fetal monitor, my baby would get the hiccups.

"How can this child know what is going on?" The nurses were getting impatient but there certainly wasn't anything I could do about it. "Why does he have the hiccups every single time? He must be very sensitive!"

"I told him to do that so you would have to stay with me longer. Do you have any idea how lonely and boring it is in this room by myself?" They would chuckle and appreciated my position.

I was also diagnosed with gestational diabetes and had to have my blood sugar checked ten times a day. My fingertips were getting pretty sore from all the needle pricks but it was something to do rather than just lie on that bed.

This was a training hospital. Twice a week the doctor would bring at least ten students with him to examine me. I felt like a specimen under observation and certainly lost any inhibitions I might have had. It was very uncomfortable at first but I got used to it and looked forward to the student visitors.

"One of the problems mothers who have gestational diabetes may have to deal with is the baby's lungs not developing properly. You have too much abdominal fluid and your baby is spending energy producing insulin instead of lungs."

One thing I appreciated about Dr. Effries was that he didn't sugar coat anything. He continued, "We are also concerned with your age. You are thirty-nine years old and pregnant for the first time. This can put a strain on the uterus, the placenta, and other organs. We will continue monitoring you closely."

This wasn't getting any easier to digest as he continued. "You are exceptionally large for this stage of your pregnancy and the ultrasound has shown that you are growing three very large fibroids and numerous smaller ones at a very fast rate. We do not know how much room there is left for your baby. His head is not the right shape and his belly is growing at a faster rate than the rest of his body. This is caused by the extra fluid you are carrying." They always referred to my baby as 'he' or 'him' and Paul was convinced it was a boy. I was not so sure and confided to a friend that I was quite sure it was a girl.

I was waiting for good news. "The reason you are in so much pain and having a difficult time sleeping is because your ribs have cracked from the pressure and your enormous size."

It was what every woman loves to hear – "you are too big!"

"Then, of course, there is the fact that your baby is transverse lie, which basically means he is stuck sideways and can't move."

There, that must be it! Now, for the good news.

"We are scheduling you to visit the nursery in the hospital for preemies. These babies are usually under three pounds, and we want you to be prepared for a baby that will come much too early. We also want you to be prepared in case the baby does not make it. If he does make it, there is a strong possibility that he may not be mentally or physically whole. There is also a very strong possibility that he or she may have cystic fibrosis. I am sorry to have to put it that way, but you must prepare yourself."

The tears were trickling down my cheeks. I didn't know if I could handle any more. This baby was so wanted, so loved and we had waited so long. I just could not lose this baby.

Paul visited me every evening, and I would tell him about my day and the doctor's confirming words of discouragement. Every day I would hear the negative report in one form or another. I was told to expect the worst so I would not be disappointed.

"Babe, remember that God has promised us this child. He or she is going to be perfect. You have nothing to worry about. Nothing is going to change if you worry, so just keep thanking God for this gift of life and I know it will all work out." I loved hearing those encouraging words and he had to repeat them to me every night. I was living in a negative environment where the worst scenario was expected so that I would not be given any false hope.

"Babe, remember the Bible verse God spoke to your heart many years ago. It was 'Blessed is she who believed there would be a performance of that which was promised her by the Lord.' You must hold on to that promise. God does not lie. He will perform what He promised you and this baby will be perfect. I don't care what the doctors say. Just block them and all the negativity out."

I would try to do that but being pregnant I was not in total control of my emotions.

Around the end of September, Dr. Effries informed me that they were booking me for a C section in November; and if I could make it until then, the baby should be big enough to survive outside the womb.

"I have scheduled the C section on the 4th so you be sure to hold that baby in until then!" Dr. Effries smiled. He was a tender, gentle man, more like a grandfather than a doctor.

"I will doctor, I promise!" Now I had a goal. I would concentrate on keeping my promise.

It was getting more difficult to sleep from the rib pain, and I was so uncomfortable because of my size. One of the nurses would come in late in the evening and give me a back massage. That, along with visits with Paul, Jason and Ashley was the highlight of my days. I wanted to do some cross-stitching or reading, or maybe some word puzzles, but was not able to do anything but lie on that bed. My headaches were too severe to concentrate. My diet was closely monitored because of the diabetes, and I was hungry all the time. It was difficult to watch TV. I would chat with my roommate; listen to what was going on in the hall by the nurses' station and dream of a new life outside these dingy walls. The only view of the outside world was through a small window in my room – the view was a brick wall of the adjoining building. The minutes of each day passed by slowly. Some days I threw a pity party – but no one showed up!

I could see that all the responsibility was taking a toll on Ashley. She looked tired and stressed but never complained. She was always optimistic and it was obvious every time she came to visit me, she was taking good care of Jason and my home. She would tell me what she was doing and about the different places she was taking Jason for fun.

It was 1986 and the World Expo was in Vancouver. Paul and Ashley had a great idea and presented it to Dr. Effries. They asked if they could take me in a wheelchair and spend a day at Expo. He agreed after giving them a long list of precautions and promising that at the slightest problem they would call an ambulance and get me back to the hospital. They agreed and I was so excited. I only had to wait three days, and I would be out of this place that felt more like a prison cell than a hospital room. It felt like I had been in the hospital for years.

When we arrived at the Expo grounds, we realized very quickly that being in a wheel chair had positive benefits. There were hundreds of people in line for the most-visited attractions. For each of these, there was a door for the handicapped and we were directed to it. We never had to wait in line for more than a couple minutes. I felt a bit guilty but it was short-lived. I was enjoying myself far too much.

It was wonderful to be with my family and watch Jason run and play and enjoy the day to the fullest. My day pass would expire too quickly. That night I was so exhausted, even the pain did not keep me awake.

Sundays were the only special days. Paul, Ashley and Jason would come for a visit and spend the day with me. On Sunday, October 12, they came as usual but could only stay for a little while. Paul brought his video camera and shot some footage of my big belly and our family time together.

He was headed to video-tape a friend's baby christening and Ashley was going to Expo with a friend. That meant the day would be exceptionally long and lonely for me.

When the nurse came in to give me my back rub I told her, "Tonight is the night. My baby is going to come into this crazy world tonight!"

She looked a little surprised and said "That's just wishful thinking. You are just tired of this place."

"No, I really believe my baby will be born tonight."
"But you are not scheduled for your C section for another four weeks and your baby isn't due for another six."

Somehow I just knew it was time and went to bed nervous and anxious. Doctor Effries had examined me a few days earlier and I told him, "This baby is not going to wait for the C section. He's not even going to wait for the full moon which is four days away."

"Well, young lady, you just tell him he has to because I am headed out of town for Thanksgiving weekend and won't be back for a week." He smiled that fatherly smile at me as if to say "There, there young one, I have been in this business for a long time and I am rarely wrong."

I woke up at 4:45 the next morning and had to go to the bathroom. The nurses would be angry if I attempted this alone but I could not wait. When I sat down, a rush of blood came. "Dear God, help me now. Save my baby. Help me now." I pulled the emergency cord in the bathroom and within seconds two nurses were there. It struck me strange that I was calmer than they were.

"I am going to help you back to bed. Nurse – get a doctor, NOW!"

I calmed her by saying, "It's okay. I knew my baby was coming tonight. Everything is going to be fine."

She gave me a suspicious look. "Carol, you don't seem to understand. This is not normal and there could be serious complications."

I told her "God has brought me this far through this pregnancy; He is not going to abandon me now!"

"You just be quiet now." She didn't want to hear it. She just wanted to get me into bed and comfortable before the doctor arrived. The doctor told them to get me into a delivery room – STAT. That certainly made me somewhat apprehensive. All the years of waiting for this promised child and all the problems during this pregnancy were soon to come to an end. What if the doctors were right and my baby would be born too tiny or too sick to live? I so wanted it to all be over but was terribly afraid of the next phase. It took every ounce of faith in me to trust that everything was going to turn out. It would all be over soon.

They quickly got me onto a gurney and wheeled me into a delivery room. They hooked me up to all the monitoring machines and brought me a telephone to call Paul.

"Hi honey. It's time. Our baby is coming."

"I'll get there as soon as possible. Are you going to have to have surgery? Should I have Ashley bring Jason?"

"Don't bring Jason yet. Let's see what they are planning and then we can call Ashley. Please hurry. I'm getting a little scared."

Shortly after Paul got there the doctor on duty told us. "Your baby fooled us all. He or she is ready to meet you. We have scheduled a C section for six o'clock tonight."

I was so surprised. "If he is ready, why do we have to wait so long?"

"The bleeding you had this morning is a concern for us and we want to be sure both you and the baby are strong enough for surgery so we will monitor you both for a few hours."

Paul and I ran out of things to talk about because the waiting was so difficult. Every 15 minutes the nurses would come in and check the heart monitor and give us the status. Baby seemed fine to me. I just wanted to get it over with.

"I am going to have Ashley bring Jason into Tsawwassen, and we will all be back around five. Try to get some rest." Paul kissed me gently on the forehead and left.

GET SOME REST! I was so tired of hearing people telling me to get some rest. All I have done for the past few months was rest. I wanted to do anything but rest. I watched the clock and listened to the noises around me. I could hear women screaming as they were giving birth. I heard a baby's first cry and a tear ran down my cheek.

It was challenging to believe that this drawn-out situation would rapidly be coming to an end. I would soon be in my own bed and would be able to tuck Jason into his bed once again. I missed him terribly. Shortly, I would be able to eat food that actually had flavor. New life as a family would begin.

It was 4:45 that afternoon when a nurse came into the room and announced. "It's time, Love. The doctor is ready now and we will take you to the operating room."

My heart began to pound and I looked around anxiously for Paul. They were wheeling me through the hall when I saw him and Jason. I instantly started to cry.

"What's wrong?" Paul looked concerned and very nervous.

"I am scared. I don't know what to expect." I was sobbing.

Ashley had arrived and sat in the hall with Jason. They both looked excited. Ashley appeared nervous but covered it well. I didn't want to frighten them with my tears.

Paul's voice was barely above a whisper. He took my hand and said. "Everything will be perfect. Both of you will get through this with flying colors. I will be right in there with you."

"Mr. Graham, if you want to go in there with your wife, you will need to get on some scrubs and get washed up. If you get squeamish in the operating room, there will be no one to attend to you. So tell me now if you think you might faint."

"No, I will not need any attention." I was surprised there was a slight quiver and higher pitch to his voice. I knew he was nervous but was not going to miss this opportunity.

"There is a face mask and cap for you as well." The nurse led him away and I was in a room that felt all too familiar. I had too many surgeries for endometriosis. Every time I had surgery the doctor would say, "Let's hope this time you can get pregnant before it grows back again."

The anaesthesiologist gave me a shot and within a couple minutes I couldn't feel anything from my rib cage down. Paul was able to stand right next to the bed and hold my hand.

I couldn't feel much more than some pressure on my abdomen and Paul was muttering to himself. There was a curtain across my stomach so I couldn't see what was going on. I felt like I was floating. It was such a weird sensation. I could feel the pressure of the scalpel but not feel any pain. I could hear the doctors and nurses talking but they sounded like they were in a tunnel far away. At this moment, nothing mattered. It was as though I was on a cloud gliding through the air. I think I was smiling. What felt like only seconds later, I was quickly awakened from my dazed state when the doctor said, "You got what you wanted. V is for Victory."

I didn't have a clue what he was talking about. He immediately held up my daughter for me to see and I began to sob.

"Are you all right? Is everything okay? Does it hurt?" Paul seemed uneasy.

"No, I am just so happy it is over and I have my baby girl."

It only took a couple minutes for the nurses to clean her up; and when they showed her to me, one said, "See the V on her forehead? That is for Victory. She is perfect. She was a 10 on the Apgar score. You cannot get any better than that." Later I was told that she had a birthmark on the back of her neck and her forehead in the shape of a V. It was called a stork bite and was not that uncommon. As she grew up, it was never noticeable unless she got angry and then it would appear quite pink.

"I told you everything was going to be perfect. You worried for nothing." Paul was so proud. Easy for him to say!

The doctors had been concerned she would be barely three pounds considering she was six weeks early, but Rochelle weighed in at 6.6 pounds.

"Mrs. Graham, because your baby is premature we will have to put her into the intensive care nursery. It is very important that you get your strength back as well. This has been quite the ordeal for you. They will take good care of her there and you will be able to get some much-needed sleep. They will not even wake you for feedings." The nurse condescendingly explained this to me in the recovery room.

This nurse had no idea who she was dealing with. "Are you on drugs?" I asked. "There is no way you are taking my baby from me. There is not a chance in a million that you will put my baby on formula."

The pediatrician stepped in and tried to calmly explain to me that it was for the best and I told him, "If you want to keep my baby in the nursery then put a bed in there because that is where I will be."

"Very well then," he agreed, "but if something goes wrong we will have to put her in the nursery."

"Apparently you do not know what this little girl has already gone through. Nothing will go wrong!"

Paul, Jason and Ashley were in the recovery room with me

and even though I was still feeling the effects of the epidural, I was so very much aware that I now had the family I had longed for, prayed for and believed I would once have.

I was so tired of being in that hospital and asked the doctor the next day if he would allow me to go home.

Dr. Effries explained, "Carol, you have just gone through major surgery. Most women would be happy to stay in bed and be waited on and get some sleep before having to attend full time to a new baby. You must take time to heal."

"Why are you people always pushing me to sleep? I have done little else for months. I just want to go home."

"Very well. If there are no problems, you can go home a few days early."

The third day I still had the catheter in and was anxious to have it removed and get ready to go home. Paul came to visit me and was hoping he could have me released. Suddenly, I felt this incredible pressure and buzzed for the nurse.

"I have to pee really badly. Please remove the catheter so that I can go to the bathroom."

She checked the bag and said, "It is empty."

"Either you remove the catheter or I will." I was ready to scream at her.

"Okay, it will just take a moment." She was definitely perturbed.

She helped me get to the bathroom, and I immediately passed another very large mass.

The nurse buzzed the emergency button; and before I figured

out what was going on, there were three nurses and two doctors in that tiny little bathroom.

They put a bedpan under me and I passed almost 12 ounces of blood and too many tumors to count. Some of them were extremely large and there were dozens of smaller ones. This went on for over an hour and I was getting so weak. I just wanted them to carry me back to my bed.

Finally they were able to get me back into bed. They hooked me up to three separate IVs but I wasn't frightened. I felt it was finally over and everything would be fine.

I started to feel like I was fading very quickly, like the feeling you get right before you faint, but stronger. I felt like I was going to leave my body. Then I suddenly realized I was dying. Life was escaping my body and I had no strength to get it back. I was fading rapidly and was not sure how to come back.

I remembered my little boy and my new baby and knew I had to stay focused. However, concentrating was extremely difficult. I was fading in and out of consciousness. With every available ounce of strength I reached for and tugged the sleeve of the closest nurse and said "Get Dr. Effries."

"You just need to relax. We are here to take care of you."

Paul had been on the telephone in my room waiting for them to finish with me. I turned my head and with a look of terror in my eyes I whispered, "Get Dr. Effries."

He ran out of the room to the nurses' station and grabbed the microphone from the desk. "Dr. Effries, Room 312 STAT!"

Moments later, the doctor was there. I was hardly able to

focus but remember him removing the IV from my arm quickly.

"Who put this IV in her?" I detected anger in his voice I had not heard before.

One intern said "I did, sir."

I was shocked at what happened next. Dr. Effries said, "You could have killed her. Another two minutes and she would have been gone. Pack your things; you are dismissed."

Life started to surge back into me quickly, and I learned later that the intern had given me the wrong medication. I never brought it up to the doctor, and he never told me exactly what happened. I really didn't want to know.

Chapter Ten

It was autumn – my favorite time of year. The birds had a new song and the air was crisp. I had missed an entire summer of fresh air—lying in the hospital bed and longing to be outside. Four days after giving birth, I begged Dr. Effries to discharge me. I could not tolerate one more day. I was extremely weak from the whole ordeal but I didn't care—I just wanted out of there.

"I have my niece to help take care of me and I promise to call if there are any concerns." I pleaded with him.

He spoke in a fatherly tone and his eyes reflected his kindness and compassion, "Miss Carol, I know you well enough to know that what you promise me is not necessarily what you will do. But I will make your niece promise not to allow you to overdo it - or you will end up back in here with an infection or worse."

I agreed and was released. Ashley was happy to bring Rochelle and me home; but the first thing I wanted was to get to a restaurant and eat some food that didn't taste like plastic. We stopped at a steak house, which was probably not the best choice so soon after my surgery, but my cravings got the best of me. I had almost forgotten how good food tasted.

Paul was out of town and I conveniently didn't tell him I was being released for fear he would be upset. Ashley was true to her word and made me take it easy while she continued to take care of everything at home including helping with the baby.

Three weeks after getting home from the hospital, Ashley and I were invited for dinner to my friend Chrissy's. When we walked into her home, 20 people yelled "Surprise!" I literally fell to my knees, overwhelmed by the love of friends and Ashley's ability to plan the secret baby shower. It didn't make it any easier for me to think about our eminent move.

We had not received any offers on our house, but we were feeling the pressure to move to Canada and build our life together as a family. I was pleased when I walked into Paul's office-home one day and he presented me with an idea.

"I have been looking through the newspaper and found a piece of property up the coast that we can look at this weekend. It sounds beautiful. The house is small but it sits on 15 acres with a panoramic view of Vancouver Island."

I started to get excited even though I wasn't sure how we were going to swing it financially. It certainly couldn't hurt to have a look and a day together on a family outing sounded inviting.

We got up early to catch a ferry to a place called Powell River. I had heard about it but had no idea it would take two ferries to get there. It was a cool and sunny November day and perfect for looking at property. After getting off the second ferry, it was only ten miles to

Powell River but Paul explained we were going to Lund, which was actually about 35 miles north of Powell River at the end of Highway 101.

I began to have some doubt about living so far away from civilization but kept my mouth shut. "Look first; then decide." I told myself.

Lund was a little like a ghost town with one run-down hotel, a boat launch and a gas station. The hotel housed the post office and small grocery store. It was a long way from Vancouver but rather romantic. We drove another mile and found the property. As we turned onto the driveway, I watched Paul's face. He looked elated and amazed at how beautiful it was.

Eight of the 15 acres were a nursery where several people worked to prepare bedding boxes and flowering terraces.

I thought, "I can barely keep my house plants alive. This would be a major undertaking." Still, I kept silent. Paul was enjoying himself far too much for me to burst his bubble.

We drove up a very steep hill and stopped in front of the oddest shaped house I had ever seen. It was 75% glass windows and did not appeal to me at all. Apparently, it was a geodesic dome. We were given the grand tour, which took about a minute and a half to cover the 400 square feet. There was an additional loft made for people less than three feet tall.

The entire interior was beautifully done in yellow cedar but the kitchen could hold only one person at a time. The bathroom had no door and consisted of a large closet, a sink, and a shower. I hated showers. Where was the toilet?

"It's out here." The owner smiled and pointed at an outhouse about 25 yards from the front of the dome.

"You have got to be kidding me!" I laughed, knowing we would never be living in this place and could not imagine how any family could even consider it.

The owner was anxious to show us the rest of the property, but warned us we would have to walk up the hill, as the road was not car worthy. When we got to the top, the wide-open view was breathtaking. We could see the ocean, the mountains, and Vancouver Island.

He showed us the building site and I began to dream of how wonderful it would be to have a beautiful new home on this majestic piece of property, even if it was at the end of the world.

He explained to us that he was a medical doctor and an herbalist and used the lower acreage to grow herbs. There were also dozens of fruit trees and grape vines. He was going to retire and would not need the property any longer.

All the way home, Paul talked about the property and what we could do with it and what kind of house he wanted to build. I listened but knew it was just a pipe dream. We did not have the means to build a house anytime soon.

Over the next couple weeks, Paul managed to convince the owner to take our home in Point Roberts on trade in addition to a small mortgage. He also arranged for me to rent the house back from him to give Paul time to add onto the little house in Lund and make it liveable. I became a bit more enthusiastic when I realized I would not have to move into a house about the size of my bedroom. The idea of starting a whole new life together as a family was thrilling. The wait would soon end.

People who lived in Point Roberts did a great deal of their actual living in Canada. If they wanted to go to a shopping mall, they shopped in Canada. Even going out to eat, usually meant going to Canada. So, as much as I felt defeated by Paul losing the battle with immigration, I knew that living in another country would mean very little adjustment. There was no alternative and I accepted that.

I began the overwhelming job of packing, sorting and deciding what to put into storage before moving to the new little house. I set daily goals instead of trying to do it all at once. I wished that Ashley was still there to help but she had given us about eight months out of her life and it had been time for her to go back home.

In December, Paul and Jason moved to Lund with the intention of getting the house ready for us to live in.

Around the same time we had decided to move to Lund, someone Paul had worked with in the car business approached him and asked if he would be interested in running a car leasing business. It did not matter where he lived as it was all done by telephone.

Paul agreed. He ran ads in several northern small town newspapers and did the credit applications for prospective clients. Once approved, he would lease them a vehicle. It was a good income and he was able to work from home.

It was mid-January when I asked Paul how much longer it would be before the house was ready. I was anxious for us all to be together.

"I haven't had the time to do any work on the house. This

new job is taking all of my waking hours."

"But you promised you would get a proper bathroom and bedroom built before Rochelle and I came up there." There was no way I was moving to a place with an outhouse.

I didn't realize how hard he had been working and felt he was just making excuses. "Maybe you really don't want me to move there. It doesn't seem to be very important to you."

I knew my words were hurtful, but I was alone with a new baby, living far from my husband and son and feeling pretty sorry for myself. Sometimes guilt works, I reasoned.

This started a series of conversations that always ended with Paul begging me to move there. I was getting angrier about everything and felt unappreciated and alone.

The weeks turned into months until the end of March when my landlord called to inform me that the house we were living in had sold and the new owners were taking possession the middle of April. Now what? I would have to move, bathroom or not.

Having been away from Paul for so long, I began to question if I really wanted to move to Canada. Our lives had been so problematic I wondered if it was worth another attempt at normalcy. It didn't help that I was moving to the boondocks. My doubts were weighing heavily on Paul and he could hear it in my voice when he called.

"I just don't know if I want to move to Lund. I know what you are going to say and I don't know if there is anything you can say to make me change my mind."

Paul pleaded, "I promise I will make the past up to you one way or the other. This is an opportunity to start over and raise our children in a positive environment."

I responded vaguely. I felt numb. The years of stress and fear had taken its toll on me. I wanted to go home. I wanted my parents to console me. Knowing that was not possible, I eventually conceded and continued the moving process. We would finally be together as a family and I focused on that.

It was a difficult move. I loved my home and my heart ached at the thought of leaving, despite some recent bad memories. I also had to do all the packing, sorting and lifting by myself while caring for my infant daughter. I tried to stay hopeful and focused on a new life but had to deal with a lot of anger and fear. I hired a couple young men to load the truck and set out on my new venture.

By the time I was on the ferry, I began to get excited. I would make this little house a real home. I took pride in my organizational skills and knew if anyone could make this house functional for four people, I could. I also trusted Paul that it would not be long before it would be enlarged.

I drove up the long windy driveway. On one side were terraces of fruit trees and rosebushes and on the other side were 170 bedding boxes for the nursery. There was a beautiful pond, at least a half-acre in size, with weeping willows and a Japanese style bridge across one end. It was exquisite and yes, I would make it work.

I walked into our new home and was so impressed at how clean my boys had kept it. I began the job of organizing and arranging. I knew the past was behind us and looked forward to a brighter future.

Paul and Jason were thrilled to see us. Jason wanted to show me all his treasures and proudly shared where he had stored all his toys in the house to make room for his little sister's things.

"I have missed you so much little man! I am so proud of you!" Jason beamed with pride. It was good to be home – such as it was. I was shocked to see how much Jason had grown and Paul had never looked happier.

"What have you been feeding the baby, Mommy? She is huge." Jason could not believe how much a baby could change in a few months.

As busy as Paul was at his job, it was getting more and more difficult for him to conduct the car leasing business from such a great distance. It seemed to be a trust issue. People felt more comfortable discussing it in person rather than by telephone. We started some serious thinking about building the giftware business with our contacts in China. Paul started approaching gift shops locally and in Vancouver.

One of the factories he had visited in China made beautifully hand carved wooden birds -- sitting birds, standing birds and birds in flight of every size and species.

We saw the potential of pursuing this business full time and knew that Paul needed to go back to China to solidify his contacts. The factories in China that Paul worked with were several hundred miles from civilization and telephones. It was always difficult to say good-bye to him knowing we would be out of contact until he returned home.

"Don't worry so much, Babe. I'll be home in ten days, and I'll bring presents for everyone. The time will fly by." He assured me.

Ten days came and went. Two weeks and not a word. I was trying not to worry, knowing he could not contact me until he got back to Hong Kong. When three weeks passed, I became very worried. I kept my concerns hidden from the children but felt powerless. I didn't know what to do or whom to contact.

I called everyone I could think of from churches I had attended in the past and asked them to pray for his safe return. Even though I had not kept in touch with them, I needed some prayer support and didn't know anyone well enough where I lived to confide in them. I needed strength to get through this.

An old friend from Washington called unexpectedly. "Hi, Carol. I have been praying for Paul; and as difficult as this is for me, I feel compelled to tell you what I believe happened." Her voice sounded strong and convincing.

"I believe that you can stop praying for him. He has been killed in some sort of accident."

Her words hit me like a demolition ball to my chest. It was difficult to speak. My heart was beating against my chest like someone beating a drum. It was almost audible.

I felt like screaming at her "What do you mean difficult for you to say—do you think it is easy for me to HEAR?" But, I respected her and began to wonder if there was some truth to what she was telling me.

I was able to gain composure. "No, that cannot be. I do not believe that. I would have known. You must be mistaken!"

"I am so sorry Carol but I am certain that is what happened. I didn't want to tell you but knew that I had to so you could make preparations."

We said our good-byes and I began to weep. The more I cried, the stronger I felt. The same anger that had welled up inside of me when the doctor told me years earlier to go home, suffer, and die, was driving me now.

I paced the floor with my mind racing. I knew God had not failed me. I knew my friend was severely wrong. My anger was directed at her for telling me something like that, even if she believed it to be true. Who did she think she was? Did she think she had a direct line of communication with God? Wouldn't I know in my heart if something had seriously happened to my husband?

That evening, with the water running and the kids asleep, I knew I was safe to just let all my emotions out. I cried so hard that when I got out of the shower I slipped to the floor, exhausted. I felt completely lost and abandoned. I knew I had to do something, and I had to be strong. I had no friends in the area. My family lived far away and I had become careful what I shared with my sister knowing it was difficult for her to process all the problems we'd had in the past few years.

The next morning Jason asked me "Mommy, you know everything, right?" I always kidded him that Mommy had all the answers. So, I agreed with him. "Yes, honey."

His next question took my breath away. "Do you know where Daddy is?"

Tears started to trickle down my face, and I grabbed him and held him close. "No, honey, I do not but God does. We are going to pray that he is safe and will be home soon."

That day I started making phone calls to try to locate him. The airlines would not give me any information; and when I demanded to speak to the supervisor, I was finally told that only the RCMP could get this type of information about a passenger.

I called the guest rooms and hotels he had stayed at in Hong Kong in the past. No one had seen him.

I finally contacted the RCMP and they, in turn, contacted Interpol. They told me not to worry, that they would find him; one way, or another.

I felt as though I was doing something; but at the same time, not producing any results. It was more frustrating than doing nothing.

Early one morning I woke up feeling feverish. My breasts hurt so much I could barely get dressed. I had no idea what was wrong, but knew I had to get myself to a doctor. I got the children ready and drove the 35 miles into town.

"You have a severe case of mastitis," the doctor told me. "This is not uncommon in new lactating moms but yours is in an advanced stage." He was starting to scare me.

"First of all, you need to rest and get some help with the children. You need to eliminate all stress as well."

"Doctor, you have no idea how impossible that is. My husband is missing in China, and I don't know anyone in Lund or Powell River who could help me." My eyes welled up with emotion and the fever.

"Your fever is 108 degrees. Either you get some help at home or I am admitting you to the hospital."

"And what about my children? What am I supposed to do with them?"

He had a hard time believing my circumstances but sent me back home with a prescription and my children intact.

On the trip home, I felt sicker by the minute and just wanted to get into bed. I contacted Le Leche League in Powell River to give me some tips, and they sent a woman to help me for a couple hours with the children and prepare their meals. Somehow, over the next few days I improved.

Five weeks had gone by and as much as a part of me was suggesting I give up, I knew Paul was still alive. The words of my friend telling me he was dead kept ringing in my ear. My own positive thoughts had to scream louder to block them. I had to stay strong and cheerful for the children. I knew Rochelle was too young to figure out what was going on, but also knew that she would be sensitive enough to pick up on any negative thoughts.

A sinking feeling like a weight on my chest was pulling me down into an abyss. It felt as though my face was pulled into a permanent frown and my throat hurt. I felt incapacitated and exhausted and didn't know what to do next.

My only hope was to trust that God was taking care of Paul, and he would return home safely. It helped me maintain a degree of sanity, at least on the outside. Jason was just a little boy. How could I tell him how concerned I was? How could I tell him as much as I wanted to believe his daddy was fine, it was tearing at my insides? When I looked at his little face, I had to swallow hard before speaking so I would not cry. I wanted to hold him close and sob with him. He believed me when I told him that daddy would be home soon. What if I was wrong?

It was now six weeks since Paul told me he would be home in ten days. When the phone rang, I knew before I answered it who was calling. When I heard his voice, I didn't know if I should be relieved or angry. My emotions ran rampant.

"What on earth happened? Why haven't you called? Where have you been? Do you have any idea what you put us through?"

"I am in Vancouver, and I will tell you all about it when I come home. I am too tired and too sick to explain it on the phone."

The look on Jason's face said it all. He was grinning and crying at the same time. I hugged him close. "Daddy is coming home."

"See, Mommy, I told you not to worry. I knew God was taking care of him."

That night Paul explained that after he arrived in the depths of China, he came down with a rare fever. He was too sick to move.

"I thought I was going to die. Frankly, I didn't care if I did. I don't know how, but I was taken to a small hut full of sick people. An old Chinese man helped me onto a floor mat and took care of me. I kept losing consciousness but when I was awake I could see the old man mixing a blend of herbs and hot chilli peppers. He made me eat it so I would sweat until the poison poured out of me. He also gave me some hot broth. I had no idea what I was eating but knew it was helping."

Jason listened intently to the story his daddy was telling. His eyes widened as Paul continued. "There were huge rats, the size of Chihuahuas, all over the place and some of them would crawl over me. I was hoping it was not rat soup I was drinking."

Jason laughed as he pictured his dad with rats crawling around him.

"I had no idea that six weeks passed. I thought it was only a few days. I have never been so sick or so weak." He gave us all big hugs and told us how glad he was to be home and safe.

Six weeks after Paul arrived home, I got a phone call from the RCMP. "Mrs. Graham, we are very sorry to inform you that we have not had any success in locating your husband and all our leads turned up empty. I am sorry but we have no choice but to close the case."

I didn't know if I wanted to tell them how incompetent I thought they were. I thought it best to say nothing. I hung up the phone and laughed out loud so relieved that this story had a happy ending.

Paul stayed close to home for a couple weeks while he convalesced. He took Jason fishing one day, and they discovered a lake full of hundreds of tree stumps and root systems. He realized they could be cut into wooden stands for the carved birds from China. Within a few weeks, Paul was cutting and polishing wooden stands of all shapes and sizes.

There was a house for rent close to our property that we were able to lease as a warehouse and Paul started to produce enough bird stands to start selling out of the local market. We were amazed at how quickly they sold and gift stores were reordering as fast as we could produce them.

Bob, an acquaintance of ours saw the potential this business had. He and his partner Joe owned a large warehouse, which they offered to us to use for an assembly line factory.

We accepted their offer and set up shop. Paul knew there would be a huge market in Banff, Alberta. He made the trip there with samples of our product and was not disappointed. Our first order with one gift store in Banff was $30,000. From there, it seemed to explode. The orders were coming in so fast we needed capital funds so we could order large enough shipments of birds to keep ahead of the sales. We wanted to expand the business to bring in six-foot eagles to be sold in hotels and lodges across the country. Bob and Joe could easily see the potential and offered their line of credit to bring in the stock we needed.

We hired enough people to run the factory at home and spent the summer on the road, as a family, at gift shows across the country. At the Edmonton Trade Show, we met two brothers from Toronto who were extremely impressed with the birds and wanted to be our distributors for Eastern Canada. We set up a meeting with our partners and it didn't take long to negotiate the particulars.

We knew it was virtually impossible to get into the Toronto Gift Show but were able to secure a space with these two brothers who were already booked for the show. It was successful beyond our expectations, and we sold over $50,000 in a couple days with the potential of many more orders.

I was taking care of the bookkeeping and office management. Paul had been back to China a couple more times and had a whole line of whales and fish set up as our next product line. We would use the same wooden bases that gave each piece a unique West Coast flair.

"I have made some good friends there. I can't wait to take

you and the children to China someday." It was all so exciting, and our past woes seemed so distant.

We already had enough inventory to fill the reorders that continued to come in. It was wonderful to be so busy, and we began to recall one of Paul's original reasons for going to China. It was still his dream to minister in China with John, and we knew this dream would soon be fulfilled with the continued success of this business.

"If there is anything I learned from my trips to China, it is that the Chinese people do not trust Caucasians easily; but when they do, they are very loyal to that relationship." Paul explained. "They will not even discuss an order on the telephone with anyone but me."

Our partners agreed that our investment in the partnership was our expertise, hard work, all the sales we made and our Chinese contacts. Without these, there would be no business.

After the Toronto orders were filled, we waited for our Eastern distributors to send the check. We had kept our end of the bargain, and they would reap a hefty commission. The check didn't arrive. Our phone calls and messages were left unanswered.

This could not be happening. But it did. All our efforts went unrewarded. The brothers disappeared. We had been taken, again.

When Bob and Joe called an emergency meeting, we were anxious to figure out a way to resolve this and were willing to work as hard as necessary to make up for the loss. They, however, thought otherwise. Even though they were in 100% agreement with us when we all met with the brothers from Toronto and set up the contract together, they were now blaming us for everything.

"You are totally responsible for this loss. What were you

thinking? How could you be so stupid?" The accusations flew fast and furious. We did feel responsible, of course, but no more than they should have been.

"Bob and I have reached a decision." Joe continued. "We are giving you a choice. You can stay in this partnership with one-third share in the business as an employee. You will not have a voice in any decision making and we will run all aspects of the business. Or you can leave, taking nothing out of the company, and walk away from the debt of this loss."

Paul knew their ulterior motive was to remove him from the business and reap the benefits of the growing enterprise. He took a day to think about it before giving them his answer. They had no experience in sales on any level and his contacts in China would not work with them in any capacity. He could not face working in the factory without being involved in decision making. He knew they would fail miserably so he gave them his answer.

Both of us were nauseated over this decision, but we were put in a position with no room for negotiation. We had started this business with a few six-inch birds Paul brought back from China and it had grown to a full-fledged enterprise. Now, we had to walk away with nothing.

They appeared very surprised to hear Paul say "I have chosen to walk away from the debt. You have almost $250,000 product in retail value. I know the potential of this business, but I cannot be a part of it under these circumstances."

We had no idea what we were going to do. We started by renting a truck to pick up our office equipment. When we arrived at the warehouse the next day, the locks had been changed and we were told that everything inside the office was now theirs.

My chest felt heavy and my breathing deep, but I was too desensitized to cry. Even after so many negative experiences, I was shocked at the depth of human spitefulness. This was one too many times. The life was knocked out of me. How would we survive another catastrophic blow?

Over the following days I worked hard at holding my emotions in, not allowing people to see the pain, but I felt as though I was wearing a sandwich board and wondered why no one asked me what was wrong.

I was too battle weary to explain to my sister or anyone else in my family that we were abused and our good natures taken advantage of again. We felt stupid and naive. Who would believe that we allowed this to occur again? People are supposed to learn from their mistakes, not keep making them. However, we didn't know what we could have done differently.

Within a few months, the rumors spread through the small town that the bird business was hurting. Just as Paul predicted they would fail; they did. In the meantime, in order to survive, Paul started clam digging and picking pine mushrooms to sell. He was making enough to barely get by until we could figure out our next step.

We sold our second car to help pay the mortgage. Paul used a little left-over money to buy another vehicle to sell. We started selling one or two cars a month and trusted this would get us out of the hole and on our feet again.

It was not unusual in a small town to permit someone to take a car for a test drive without going with them. So when someone made an appointment to take a car we were selling for a trial run, we had no reason to suspect any wrongdoing. When the person didn't return with the car, we discovered he was one of Bob's friends.

Bob forged Paul's name on the transfer slip and sold the car. Before calling the police to report the car as stolen, Paul called Bob.

Bob's wife answered the phone and said, "I'm sorry but Bob will not take your call."

Paul told her what her husband had done and that he was going to call the police.

"I beg you not to do that. We have small children and I can"t take care of them if Bob goes to jail. Please don't call them." She continued to cry and plead with Paul until he reluctantly promised her he would not. We realized then that if we had continued in business with Bob, we might have lost even more.

Paul saw no choice but to look for work in Vancouver—a five-hour journey and two ferry trips away. This was not supposed to happen this way. I longed to turn the clock back in time and push a restart button on my life. There was no button, this was reality.

Within a few days, he was able to secure a car brokerage job, which he really enjoyed. He would buy a fleet of cars from one dealership and sell them to another. Basically, he lived in his car putting about 10,000 miles a month on the odometer. He loved sales and was once again in his element, but he was only able to make it home one weekend a month. It was especially hard on the children.

I was home schooling Jason while Rochelle would play school right along with us. Paul's mother came for a visit and could not believe we were living in such a tiny house without a bathroom.

"You are so busy with the children but I know you, Carol. You need to do more. I think you should start a Christian Woman's Club (CWC) in Powell River."

"What in the world is a Christian Woman's Club?" She had tweaked my interest.

"Christian Woman's Club is an international organization. It is interdenominational and a great outreach to women of all faiths. I love my club in Alberta. Once a month, we have luncheons and provide entertainment for the women. Each time, someone shares her life story of how God has worked in her life." She promised to send me materials on how to start one in Powell River.

"I love the idea of fashion shows, and music and various how-to demonstrations that appeal to women from all walks of life." Once again, Mom had given me a fantastic idea.

I contacted every church in Powell River and began recruiting women to help. It took almost a year to get it organized, but I was so proud and pleased at the result. Our first month we had over 200 women attend, and it was fun, refreshing, and fulfilling. The reception in the community was fabulous. I worked with about 20 women to plan and organize each month's luncheon, and we had a great time making each one interesting and unique.

In order to bring in some extra money, I decided to restart my dessert business. There was no conceivable way I could run the business out of my tiny kitchen so I approached a friend I met through CWC. I offered her half the profit for her assistance and the use of her kitchen. She jumped at the chance, and I took out my original menu of desserts.

I started with the largest restaurants in town and was well received. Within a few days, I had three solid commitments and we began our venture.

Home schooling can be done anywhere so the kids would come with me to Donna's house three days a week. We put in full days and made a lot of desserts. As much as I missed Paul, I was so busy there wasn't much room for feeling lonely or sorry for myself.

The most difficult part of this new lifestyle was it was precisely what we had come here to avoid. We were to be a family living together, as normal families do. But circumstances forced our lives to take a different direction.

So much of my time was spent driving back and forth to Powell River. It was 30 minutes each way. The weekly CWC meetings, any and all shopping, home school activities, church activities, and working the dessert business all required me to be on the windy, narrow, one-lane highway.

It was common to see the big logging trucks on the highway and always a bit unnerving when approaching one of them on an oncoming curve.

One day I was deep in thought, making plans and to-do lists, when I saw two of the eight front tires of a logging truck disengage and roll towards me with a deafening rumble like steamrollers gaining speed. There was no time or place to swerve out of the way. I cried out "Help me God!" What happened next defies all laws of nature.

Even though I was still driving, it felt as if I were sitting still. In a matter of a split second, the two gigantic tires speeding towards me separated just in time to pass by on either side of my car.

My hands shook as I found a place to pull over. I looked back and realized the trucker had stopped his rig on the highway. I jumped out of my car and starting running back. He was getting out of his truck and I yelled at him." Are you okay?"

"Yes, are you?"

"Yes, I am. I think the angels were looking out for me."

"In all my years as a truck driver, I have never seen anything like this." He was wiping his brow as if the shock of what he just witnessed made him perspire.

I quickly got back in my car and thanked God for His protection of both the trucker and myself. It was an experience I did not soon forget.

We continued to live in our cozy but very tiny house, which still lacked a completed indoor bathroom. Paul had built a shed close to the house for a washer and dryer which was a huge improvement. It meant I no longer had to take the laundry into Powell River.

From the time Rochelle was born until she was nine months old, she had projectile vomiting every time she ate. I would nurse her and then ever so gently try to lay her in her bed but no matter how careful I was, she would throw up her food with a vengeance. Most days I had to change my clothes at least five times and hers even more often. It was exhausting, so having a washer and dryer in the shed was a huge blessing.

The waterline to the house had never been buried properly and extended up the hill from the water main. Every winter, as soon as it came close to freezing, we had problems. The hill was mostly rock, so there really was no way to bury it without putting in a whole new system. We had to leave the water tap dripping so it would not freeze, but it was difficult for the children to remember and I forgot many times as well.

Sometimes we went days without running water, depending on the temperature outside. The line usually froze when Paul was gone. Jason and I would try our best to get it thawed out but often to no avail. I shed a lot of tears over it. As breathtakingly beautiful as this property was, I began to hate living in Lund more each year. The problems outranked the beauty.

It was close to Christmas and snowing. It was the day of our CWC Christmas luncheon, and we had a lot of festive activities and surprises for the ladies. I left the house early in the morning to supervise the setup. Paul was home with the children.

I was driving slowly and carefully in my 4x4 Bronco; being especially cautious as I approached a curve or the crest of a hill. Then, out of nowhere, directly in front of me was a car stopped in the middle of the road. I had three choices. I could swerve around it on the left into the curve and a rock wall, I could swerve to the right, take the ditch and possibly go over the cliff, or I could rear end the car. In a fleeting second I decided to swerve to the left.

The Bronco was light and had large tires. When I swerved, it flipped end-over-end two times. I remembered seeing cars in the movies that rolled over side-to-side, but I had never seen one roll end-over-end. As the Bronco started into the first roll, I felt as though I was flying in slow motion. It continued into its second roll, and I knew that I had no control over whether I lived or died. I cried out loud "NO!" The second cry was louder than the first "NO!" and the truck landed upright facing the opposite direction. I had survived but did not realize the impact I'd taken.

All the windows were smashed as well as the six empty glass milk bottles in the back seat. The back tailgate was thrown open, and I crawled out the back without realizing I had no shoes on. The entire inside of the truck was littered with broken glass, yet I escaped without a cut.

The lady who had stopped her car pulled over and came running to me.

"Are you all right? I am so sorry. Two dogs were crossing the road and I stopped for them."

"Are you crazy?" I screamed at her. "Do you realize you could have killed me or both of us?"

"I wasn't thinking." She tried to put her arm around me.

"Get my shoes. My feet are freezing. I have a meeting to get to."

"But you're hurt. I need to get you to a hospital."

I would hear none of it. I continued to shout orders to her and made her crawl into my truck and get all the gifts and totes I had for the luncheon.

She said she lived in Lund as well, and she would take me home and then call a tow truck to get my Bronco. It was out of the way of oncoming traffic, and I was determined to get to the luncheon. We argued about it, but I started to feel the pain of the accident and agreed to let her take me home.

Once there, I changed my nylons, which had several runs in

them. I looked in the mirror and saw a huge goose egg developing in the center of my forehead but otherwise I was pretty much intact. I detected a lot of small particles of glass in my hair but I left it alone. Time was wasting and we had to make the trip back into town. It would take close to an hour as it was snowing heavily and had been for some time. The luncheon started at noon and it was already 11:30.

Paul was noticeably upset. His voice was shaking as he tried to comfort me. I was more concerned that I had smashed our means of transportation. The children just stared at me and didn't say a word. I think they were scared. I was so determined to get back to town I told them I was fine. They didn't question it.

The lady drove me back to town, and I invited her to stay for the luncheon. When I walked in, everyone was eating and several other ladies had looked after all the preliminaries. When they saw me, everyone stood up and clapped. I was totally embarrassed and assured them I was fine.

Throughout the rest of the luncheon, my goose egg continued to grow, and I started to hurt all over. I was able to find someone to drive me home and looked forward to getting the glass out of my hair and lying down in some comfy pajamas.

On the trip home, in almost the exact location of the accident, the lady driving me slid into the ditch and got stuck. I wasn't thinking rationally and I got angry with her.

She ignored my anger and got out of the car to wait for someone to come by who could contact the police or a tow truck for us. It took almost two hours before help arrived. It was dark by the time I finally got home. I broke down and wept.

The Bronco had been my only means of transportation, and we had no insurance. It was just another hurdle to get over. Paul was home for the Christmas season and that was good. The New Year was always promising.

It was the early nineties and the economy had taken a down turn. The car business was hit hard. Paul was putting in about 16 to 18 hours a day with very few sales. A lot of his associates had resorted to living on borrowed money; a luxury we did not have. My dessert business had slowed down as well. Not as many people were eating out and people were more aware of their waistlines than in the past.

Paul was coming home less than before. Each ferry trip cost about $100, and we just could not afford it. Even though I was trying to stay positive, I felt like Lund was a prison, and I was sentenced to life. I wanted out. I talked to Paul about it, but he was looking to a brighter future. He still believed we could make it work and that something would turn around for us. I was not so optimistic. I felt trapped. Discouragement told me that we were never going to leave Lund. We would always be in this excuse for a house with all its problems. It was an ongoing battle to keep positive.

Chapter Eleven

I had heard my share of sermons built around the subject of trusting God's ways rather than our own. But this is not easy when those you've trusted so many times have betrayed you. I was even having a difficult time trusting our own decisions. Still, we knew God would never fail us and would give us the strength to go forward.

One of the main reasons we moved to Lund was to be together as a family, yet we were only seeing Paul about one weekend a month. He was working seven days a week and we were barely making ends meet. It felt like we were drowning in a sea of debt without a lifeline. I missed him so much. I missed living as a family and was so incredibly lonely.

Our living conditions were embarrassing and I could not foresee any change in the near future. I was never officially diagnosed but believed I suffered some sort of "snap." Experts would certainly use fancier language to describe when someone goes over the edge. It can happen in a split second as a result of a traumatic event. Or, it can be the final straw, the culmination of pressure that builds until the mind and body must find a release. I believe this is what was happening to me. I had a difficult time functioning in my daily routine. I felt as though a black cloud had overtaken me, and I would never break through. I was overwhelmed by my present circumstances and the relentless past. I lost my appetite and had a difficult time sleeping.

As hard as it was, I knew I had to pull myself out of depression and change my focus. So, rather than regret what happened or regard the past six years as a complete waste of time, I began to analyze and accept what I had learned from the struggle. I forced myself to reflect on the positives and to be proud for starting a Christian Woman's Club in our area. It continued to grow and be a vital asset to the community, and I had made good friends from those connections. Still, it was not enough to make me want to stay in Lund.

My list of reasons for moving was growing. Living in a larger community within a short distance to stores, school and church sounded wonderful. I wanted a real house, with a real bathroom, not an outhouse. I hated showers and longed for a bath. We had no running water during the cold winter months or a telephone that worked when it rained. A bedroom of our own was a dream.

At first, these seemed like minor issues but they were becoming major ones. It had been almost seven years and I had had enough. If Paul had been living with us full time, it may have been different but with no local jobs and no money to start any kind of business venture, it was impossible.

I had to convince Paul to sell and "get out of Dodge." I tread carefully into this tender area knowing he had such big plans for the property, and I felt guilty asking him to put my desires ahead of his.

To my surprise and relief, he agreed wholeheartedly. I had been thinking only about myself but his response told me that life in Lund had been difficult for him too.

We called a real estate agent and put the property up for sale. Paul spent some days at home working on the bedding boxes and the Alders that had tried to take over the pond area.

The pond was one thing we knew the property had going for it. A few months earlier, Jason and our Husky, Sheba, had made a great discovery.

"MOM, come quick!" Jason shouted from the front deck.

There stood Sheba breathing heavily and wagging her tail with great pride.

"Look what Sheba brought home!" It was a beautiful orange Koi weighing about eight pounds. Sheba had brought this up to us from the pond, which was about five acres from the house. She carried this large fish up a very steep hill to plant it on our deck.

"Show me where you got this." Jason followed her down the trail to one edge of the shallow pond.

We researched these fish and discovered Koi of this size could be very valuable. We hired a diver to go into our pond, and he discovered it was actually about 25 feet deep and dense with Koi of every size. We were excited to learn that some of these fish were worth several hundred dollars each. We used this as a selling feature.

I was delusional enough to think someone would immediately buy this property, and we could leave Lund and start a new life closer to civilization. I began making plans and alerting CWC members and friends of our decision.

In reality, no one even came to inspect the property until seven long months later when I received a phone call from a woman in Vancouver. She was very interested in opening a retreat center for recovering Heroin addicts. We had instant rapport and she made an appointment to view the property.

She fell in love with it as soon as she arrived. It was perfect for what she wanted to develop and we completed the sale.

Things started to fall into place quickly, and I was terribly excited at the potential of actually moving. I was a little worried because the children had made friends and loved living in the wilderness, but I hoped they were young enough to adjust to the move easily.

A couple weeks earlier I had driven to Sechelt, which was one ferry closer to Vancouver, in anticipation of finding a place to rent. It was difficult to believe but the newspaper had only one house for rent and the ad stated no pets or kids.

I called the landlord, who lived in Vancouver, and managed to convince him to let me see the place even after I told him we had two kids and two pets. The neighbor had the key and would let me in.

It was the middle of summer and the yard was beautiful. It was not manicured, but rustic with lots of trees and shrubs and a big garden area. The house was tucked into the woods at the end of a long driveway. It had two floors, three bedrooms, and indoor plumbing. This was the perfect place for us.

I called the landlord back and told him we would take it but it turned out he had been kind enough to let me see the place but had no intention of renting it to us. I talked to him for about 15 minutes and convinced him we would look after his house as if it was our own. I told him I guaranteed his house would be in better condition when we moved out then when we moved into it. He finally agreed and I was so relieved not to have to look any further.

Things were rapidly turning around for us. We could start over with money in the bank and the potential of better things to come. I felt rewarded for always trying to maintain a good attitude and believed we could only go uphill from here.

We rented the largest truck available and offered the job of loading it to some of the men in the neighborhood. Most of them were not working, other than digging for clams or picking pine mushrooms, so they appreciated some extra cash.

One thing we particularly wanted to take with us was a beautiful mirrored cedar cabinet. It had been built inside the dome and never had gone through the front door. It was about seven feet long and six feet high with mirrors and drawers. There was no way to disassemble it, but Paul was determined he and the other men would make it fit through our triangular shaped front door. It took five of them almost three hours but they managed to do it, with no broken mirrors. We were finally on our way to a new home and a new life with $50,000 in the bank from the sale of our house and high hopes of finding a new one very soon.

Finally we were ready to head to the ferry. Paul, Jason and Rochelle were in the big truck and I followed in the car. Paul carefully drove down the steep hill and around those tight curves. He was just turning onto the highway from our driveway when the rear tires slid into a deep ditch. What happened next defied reason and gravity. It was as if an unseen force picked up the rear of the truck and placed it onto the highway. I could hardly believe my eyes.

I began to cry and by the time we got a mile down the road I was weeping so hard I could not drive. I had to pull over. Paul noticed in his rear view mirror and pulled over too. He walked swiftly to my car and as I rolled down the window he asked, "What's wrong, honey?"

"What happened back there? Did you see it? An angel picked up the back end of the truck!"

"Yes, I know. I didn't see it but I felt it. But there is something else wrong, isn't there?"

"I am just so happy and relieved to leave this place. It almost destroyed us, especially our marriage, and I never want to see this hell hole again." I was angry, anxious, and so very tired. Not just tired from the day -- but just exhausted!

"I know it has been really rough on all of us. But things will be different now. We have a fresh start and everything will work out, you'll see." Just hearing that encouragement gave me new strength.

We arrived at our new home around 11 o'clock that night and decided to bring in mattresses and make some beds on the floor. The rest could wait.

Both Jason and Rochelle had their own rooms and the master bedroom was as big as our whole house in Lund. We especially appreciated an indoor bathroom. I was looking forward to the fun of arranging everything and cooking in a real kitchen.

On our second morning, I was very shocked to see Paul come down the stairs dressed up and announcing, "I have to go out of town for a few days."

"What are you talking about? Where are you going?"

He was very evasive and basically said he had to get back to work. Now that we were living closer to Vancouver, it was my understanding that he was going to commute daily. I was certainly not expecting him to go away for a few days without discussing it with me first.

A few days turned into a week and I had no idea where he was. When he called, I was not expecting him to be on the other side of the country.

"Hi Honey. I am in Winnipeg for a few days."

"What do you mean you are in Winnipeg for a few days? What are you doing there?" Now I understood why he had been ambiguous.

"Remember my buddy Bruce? He told me there was a car auction in Winnipeg, and I could get cars dirt cheap and turn them over for a quick profit. So, I came here to check it out and he was right."

I felt like I was in some kind of imaginary state. I could not possibly be hearing him correctly. I thought he was in Vancouver at work. I was afraid to ask the inevitable question.

"How much did you spend?"

His hesitation in answering was answer enough. He must have spent the entire amount from the sale of our house. I wanted to believe him. I also wanted to shoot him. I had no choice but to trust him. We said our good-byes and I didn't hear from him again for several days.

During this time, I had thought long and hard about the entire situation and the longer I thought about it, the angrier I got. How dare he? How could he do this? What if he lost money instead of making a profit? My thoughts ran rampant and I couldn't sleep. Finally he called and he sounded great.

"Paul, I am only going to say this once. Either you get home in the next couple days or you will not have a home to come to." I was surprised at the staccato tone in my voice but I meant every word.

He must have sensed it as well. "I will be home immediately." We hung up and I was shaking; partly from anger and partly from fear.

As promised, Paul was home in two days and reassured me that he had done this for our future. He promised we would double our investment. I believed him until I discovered he had bought sports cars. It was August; and if we had been able to hold onto them until the spring, it may have been profitable. The deals were good, but the timing was bad. We lost money. My hopes for the future were waning thin.

I started to attend one of the local churches. The people were friendly and I felt at home. My first Sunday there, I met Sandy and it felt like we had known each other forever. I knew she would be a good friend. That same afternoon, she called me, crying.

"I just don't know what to do. I cannot live like this anymore." She continued her story of her new husband not accepting her children and the way she disciplined them. They were fighting a lot and she needed a place to stay.

"You are certainly welcome to come over and we can talk about this. Bring the girls."

Shortly after, she arrived with daughters and luggage intact. They stayed about three days, and I was able to help her look at things a bit more objectively. It felt so good to be needed. I was going to like it here.

We also met Jeff at the church. He had a local car dealership in Sechelt. Paul explained to him that while we were in Vancouver we sold a fleet of cars way too cheap so we bought a few more to sell hoping to make a profit. Jeff then offered to help us out by putting some of our cars on his lot on consignment. Selling them locally seemed like a great idea.

Paul continued to work in Vancouver but the car brokering business was failing. It seemed like the bottom had fallen out of the market and there was very little work. We needed to sell the vehicles we had in Sechelt as soon as possible so agreed to have Jeff auction them for us in Vancouver, even if it meant a loss.

I was anticipating good news when Paul came home from Vancouver and certainly did not expect him to tell me, "Jeff won't pay me for the cars!"

"What do you mean he won't pay you for the cars?"

"In order for him to wholesale the cars at the dealer's auction, they all had to be in his name. So, I gave him the titles and now he won't pay me. He claims they were his."

It was late evening and the kids were asleep. I was standing in the kitchen when he told me this, and I felt as though the ground beneath my feet might simply cave. I slowly began to slide down the side of the cupboards as my legs were incapable of holding me up.

I curled up and began to weep, almost hysterically. Paul stood there for a minute or so and then said, "Don't expect me to help you. I have nothing left to give." That knife went straight into my heart. I had expected him to tell me it was all going to be okay.

I just did not have the energy to get up from the floor and spent most of the night there crying a lot but also getting furious.

Mornings always seem to make life appear better and brighter without the hopeless feelings of the night before. I tidied myself up and roused the children. Paul left for Vancouver to go back to work and to stay for a while. He had met someone in the car business that he could stay with. He said it would cut down on expenses by not traveling back and forth every day.

I knew that forgiveness was a choice. I could remain aggravated and accomplish very little, or I could choose to forgive and move forward. I chose to forgive and focus on the future.

I decided to place my children in the Christian school associated with the church we were attending. I was offered a job in the office in exchange for their tuition. It was thrilling to feel needed, and I appreciated and enjoyed my new job.

We saw less and less of Paul. He didn't make it home each weekend as was expected. In fact, he only made it home a couple of weekends a month. Business was picking up, and he wanted to put in as many hours as possible. I was making new friends from the school and church, but I kept our past in the past. I did tell them about my healing and our miracle baby, but I did not have the energy to share the other things that had happened. I wanted to feel normal and fit in.

CWC contacted me and asked if I would be interested in being a speaker for them. It would mean traveling around British

Columbia telling my life story on a circuit of five to seven luncheons in a row. I jumped at the chance, knowing I had a lot to share that would encourage women who related to my experiences. I would share my belief that no matter what happens in life, God is always there to pick you up and give you the strength to carry on.

I would require babysitters for the children for the weeks I would be gone but it was important enough to me to work it out. Over the next ten years, I traveled to a lot of communities and was often asked to return.

When I shared how good God had been to me and how blessed I was, it encouraged me. When I talked about my restored health and my precious children, it reminded me of what really mattered. As difficult as the financial struggle had been, nothing could take away the joy of God's blessing.

At home, the children and I worked at making Paul's infrequent visits special. I made his favorite meals and desserts, planned outings and allowed him time to relax away from the busy city and stressful work schedule.

But, I began to feel like a single parent. A lot of the decision making and problem solving in raising the children was on my plate. Jason became the young man of the household. He chopped wood for the fireplace, helped with the yard work and anything else I needed. Both he and Rochelle were making new friends at church and school.

I was still pursuing my Shaklee business and helping people with their various health issues. On the weeks I was not traveling, I conducted group meetings to share what I had discovered in the wellness arena. When clients heard my story, they wanted to experience the same vitality and good health. I took as many nutritional courses as I could by home studying in the evenings and did the necessary research to help people with individual issues. It was tremendously rewarding to see so many people turn their health around.

Keeping busy helped make the time go quickly between Paul's weekends home. I know he missed us a lot and was working diligently to pull us out of our current situation.

One of my friends from church was about to have a baby and asked me to coach her in her birthing experience. The baby's father was not currently in her life, and she didn't have a birthing coach. It was a last minute request a few days before she went to the hospital, but I jumped at the opportunity to see a birth and be part of something so incredible.

Fortunately, Paul was home the evening she called to tell me it was time to come to the hospital. I was in the middle of preparing dinner and hurrying to finish it before leaving for the hospital, when there was a loud knock at the front door sounding more like a thud than a knock.

"Jason... please see who is at the front door!" I called.

I heard him open the door, and then quickly slam it shut.

Running into the kitchen he shouted "Mom, you won't believe this! There was a huge bear on the porch!"

"Are you all right?" I was grateful he looked unscathed.

"I'm okay Mom. I just locked the door." Sounded logical to me. I assumed the bear smelled the dinner cooking and wanted to join us.

I spent several hours at the hospital. I had never personally experienced labor and didn't know it could take so long. I tried to be a good nurse but was running out of things to talk about and could only bring her so many ice chips. Around midnight I called home.

"Sorry, honey, but it looks like I will be spending the night at the hospital."

Paul did not respond and I realized his breathing was heavy and labored.

"What's wrong? You sound terrible. Are the children okay?"

"I... am... okay, just a bit shaken. You won't believe what just happened. I let the cat out to relieve himself and the light from the porch illuminated a pair of eyes in the distance. I stepped out onto the deck to see what it was and before I had taken two steps, the largest cat I've ever seen lunged towards me.

I did not realize the potential danger he had been in, until he continued.

"It all happened so fast. The cougar was literally in midair when I shouted at it. I was going to say 'in the name of Jesus get out of here.' All I had time to say was 'In the name...' it did a 180-degree turn in mid-air and disappeared. It was absolutely unbelievable. That cat had full intention of attacking me. God totally protected us." As he shared what happened, he began to calm down.

When I called home the next morning, Paul told me that when he went outside he noticed our leather dog collar that had been hanging by the back door was missing. He found it in the yard where he first noticed those eyes in the darkness. It terrified us to think that cat had come onto our deck, took our dog collar off the door handle, and into the yard to chew on it. What if the door had been open?

"I called the conservation officer who told me they had been tracking one of the largest cougars that had ever been seen in this area, and he was sure it was the same one." Paul still sounded shaken and it frightened me to think about what could have happened.

My friend gave birth that morning; and I was made more aware than ever of the awesomeness of God, our creator, and our protector.

Over the next few months I began exercising and was proud of myself for losing weight and fitting into my skinny jeans again. That was soon to change dramatically. One morning when I was lying in bed I knew something was seriously wrong. My abdomen felt rock hard.

I saw a specialist and finally, several months and many tests later, I got a diagnosis: tumor. Tumor is a word that conjures up all kinds of emotion – mostly fear. Suddenly I was thrown back 25 years and I was sitting across the desk from the doctor who told me I had cancer. How could this be happening? I was healthy – healthier than ever in my life. My heart felt constricted and I struggled just to breathe and think clearly.

I decided what I needed was an intense program of diet and supplementation designed to get rid of this invader. I was confident this tumor would soon disappear. A local naturopath had me doing a series of techniques that stopped just short of standing on my head in an attempt to have this growth break free. I was beginning to look about 11 months pregnant and feeling more awful and ugly each day. I assumed that anyone who looked at me would either think I was very fat or very pregnant. I did not like the way people stared at me. My self-esteem was dropping rapidly. My family doctor was concerned that a rapidly growing tumor could turn to cancer if not removed.

My mother was in her forties when I was conceived. She discounted her pregnancy because of her age and for seven months she thought she had a tumor. I was beginning to wonder if history was repeating itself and this growth might actually bear hair and teeth.

I was desperate and sought the advice of a world-renowned naturopath in Oregon. He assured me the only alternative was surgery, with a tumor this large. It was just too large to attempt to pass it naturally. However, surgery posed two major problems. I did not have any medical insurance and any doctor I consulted felt it was just too risky to attempt removal.

X-rays showed that it had adhered itself to several organs including my heart, colon, and liver. I was told there were hundreds of arteries leading to this mass, which were using most of my nutrition and causing a serious threat to my circulation.

The circulation in my arms and legs had screeched to a halt. I could barely walk up the stairs. Even removing clothes from the dryer left me feeling faint. My limbs felt like spaghetti. The sheer enormity of it made it difficult to breathe. Getting in and out of a vehicle was hard work. Walking any distance or exercising was out of the question.

Finally, my research paid off; I found a doctor in New York who would remove it for $25,000. Where would I get that kind of money? But, did I have any other choice?

It seemed I did. My family doctor finally contacted me

because he found a gynecologist who was also a general surgeon. He had experience with large life-threatening tumors. He was from Texas but performed surgery in Vancouver for special cases.

I was very nervous waiting to see this miracle worker. I had carried this tumor around for almost three years, and it was estimated to weigh 15 pounds. The doctor must have sensed my anxiety.

"Mrs. Graham, I can only imagine how much you want to have this growth removed. I have performed this type of surgery several times, and I want you to rest assured that every precaution will be taken to be sure it is removed safely and in its entirety. Unfortunately, we must also perform a complete hysterectomy at the same time to be sure it never grows back."

I still had many questions and one of them was the cost. This doctor took pity on me and said that he would only charge $600 for his portion. I could hardly believe my ears.

"However, you will need a minimum of five days of hospital recovery time. This is a very serious surgery and until I see inside I will not know exactly what is involved. There could be serious ramifications and I cannot take any chances. This is unusual and unknown territory."

I was a bit disappointed to hear of the long hospital stay and did not sleep well thinking about how I was going to pay for all this.

The hospital required their payment up front. I almost fainted when they quoted me $2,500 per day. I needed an alternate plan.

I made another appointment with the surgeon and inquired of him, "I really do understand how serious this situation is and that this tumor has to come out. However, I cannot afford $13,000. I am strong and determined, and I am begging you to find a way that I can leave the hospital 24 hours following surgery. How can we make this happen?"

He realized I was serious and reluctantly agreed under certain conditions.

"The only way I will agree to this is if you are able to eat food and keep it down within that 24 hour period. You will also have to stay in the area for three days. There is a hotel across the street and if there are any complications, you will be only a few minutes away."

Of course I agreed. We booked a hotel room. It certainly did not cost $2,500 a day and was definitely more pleasant than the hospital. So my journey to recovery began.

I was admitted at 7:47 A.M. and knew how crucial it was to leave before this time the next day. The nurses were on strike which was causing a great deal of delays and certainly added to my list of concerns. I was prepped and quite nervous. Paul held my hand and joked that I would be jogging in a few days.

My surgery was scheduled for 1:00 P.M. I was watching the clock and was very antsy wondering why everything was taking so long. The longer it took, the shorter recovery time I had before being released. Finally, in the operating room, I was asked to count backwards from ten. I counted to seven and that's the last thing I remember.

Paul told me later how difficult it was to wait the hour and half until the doctor announced to everyone in the waiting room, "I just removed a tumor the size of a basketball." The doctor hesitated and then made a motion with his hands to show the size of a basketball and then corrected himself.

"No, rather it was more like a beach ball." Paul said he smiled in a boyish manner and seemed proud in a strange sort of way. The room went quiet in disbelief. Paul watched some jaws drop but instant relief swept over him. He knew the rest would be good news!

I had made Paul promise to wake me very early the next morning no matter how drugged I was. I had to have my wits about me to get released by 7:47 A.M.

What an awful night. I was thrown into instant menopause with an endless hot flash. The nurses kept covering me up which was extremely irritating as it was difficult to remove the blankets in my post-surgery condition. I was sweating profusely. What was wrong with them?

I kept removing the oxygen mask to prepare for my dismissal but could not breathe on my own. I was frightened but even in my drowsy state, very determined. I kept watching the clock in and out of consciousness and remembered that Paul promised he would be there in plenty of time to get me out before 7:47 A.M. He arrived around 6:30 A.M. I was in no shape to leave. I could barely move, much less walk. I was hooked up, taped up, spaced-out, and weak.

I buzzed for the nurse and told her I had to use the bathroom as I would be leaving soon. She laughed. I was not in a laughing mood.

"I'm serious. I need help to the bathroom, and I need my breakfast immediately as I will be leaving here shortly."

"You are not going anywhere, Ma'am. I will get a bed pan for you."

"You do not seem to understand. I am leaving here in about

30 minutes with or without your help."

She wasn't laughing anymore and seemed quite agitated. I asked Paul to get the doctor.

He asked the head nurse at the station to please bring my breakfast as soon as possible and to alert my doctor that I was ready to be released. Breakfast was delivered around 7:00 A.M. There was no way I could eat an egg and toast.

"Babe, you are going to have to eat this." Paul saw the desperate look in my eyes.

Paul was concerned but knew I was determined to leave as planned so he quickly ate it for me. That accomplished, I knew the doctor had been paged so he could release me. Minutes were ticking by quickly and I was NOT going to be late. It would mean another $2500.

My doctor came in but I was in such a haze I didn't even recognize him.

"Good morning, Mrs. Graham, I see you have had your breakfast." I admitted nothing.

"I have good news and bad news. The good news is that I am releasing you seeing that you were able to keep your breakfast down. The bad news is that when I was trying to remove the tumor, it was impossible to do so without pulling and cutting it. I had to use such force that I cut myself inside of you and had to put both of us through an AIDS test. I will let you know the results within a few weeks."

I didn't totally comprehend what he was saying but it didn't sound like a big problem.

"I had to tie off over 150 arteries by hand. It was the healthiest and largest tumor I have ever seen – definitely one for the books. A few of the arteries were very large and the main one was as big as my arm. It is amazing you survived as long as you have."

I knew it was amazing, and I knew it had to be pretty awful from the problems it had caused me the past couple years. But I also knew I had to get out of there!

Paul got me a wheel chair and we maneuvered down to the admission desk. I must have been a pretty sight. We paid for my one-day stay and the admission nurse was visibly upset that I had been released. I felt like I was escaping from an institution. But soon we were out the front door and free. With each inch I traveled in the wheel chair, I stifled a scream. The pain killers were not strong enough for the bumps and movements.

Paul had to help me into the car, and I thought I would pass out from pain and weakness. We drove the few blocks to the hotel and then had to get out of the car and into the elevator. I had to walk as there was no wheel chair available. After what seemed like forever, I was in the room and getting prepared for bed. It was wonderful to note that I would not have to move again for a couple days.

I knew how important it was to rest but this was virtually impossible as I began to itch from my scalp to the bottom of my feet. I could not lie still or reach most of the places to relieve the itching. I was in tears from the pain and the itching. Paul contacted the doctor to see what was happening to me, and he said it was probably an allergic reaction to the morphine. There was nothing I could do and it would take some time for it to get out of my system. So, my days of rest turned into torment but eventually the itching subsided and it was time for the trip home.

The doctor had given me a list of what I could eat and basically it was broth and some soft food. I was not having any problems with body functions and knew that it was safe to go home. It was still quite difficult getting in and out of the car and trying to hold my stitches in over the bumps in the road.

I was told to convalesce for six weeks but I have never rested that long in my entire life for any reason so I was back at work by day seven, still physically sore but with an alert mind.

With God as my strength, the tumor was gone, and I was on the road to health once again.

Chapter Twelve

Ibecame a master at avoiding questions about myself. I had done it for so many years it was second nature to me. When someone asked me, "How are you doing?" I would answer the question with another question. "How are YOU?" was my general response. I found that most people liked to talk about themselves and didn't even notice. I was able to keep my past hidden and not have to comment about any current woes. Long-term friends knew very little about me, and I liked it that way. But, often I would have preferred to just blurt it all out and tell them that life had been tough or I was going through a real rough patch but old habits die hard.

A few times over the years, those who got close to me began to realize that I avoided sharing. If they were bold enough to tell me that I should share how I am really feeling, they would. "Carol, I know that you have had a lot of pain in your life. You need to talk about it. There are areas that need to be healed." I would smile and agree but didn't go any further. I had buried much of the past deep enough that it would require too much energy to start digging it up. Disappointment became a way of life. It was easier not to get excited about anything. It made the letdown more tolerable. I assumed that few would guess what was really going on. I believed that letting my guard down would only be a sign of weakness so I protected myself with silence.

When I started speaking for CWC, I began to expose small portions of my past, being careful to protect myself from judgement or scrutiny. Sharing my life with strangers who I would probably never see again felt safe.

The opportunity to speak at CWC was becoming more frequent. I was thoroughly enjoying sharing my story and encouraging women from all walks of life to realize that no matter what life hands them, with God they will have the strength and the wisdom to deal with it.

We worked it out so that either Paul would be home or my friend Sandy would take care of the children. Whatever city I spoke in, the Club put me up in a very nice residence of one of the local members. It was like a mini vacation, being pampered and catered to. The women who hosted me had no idea how much I appreciated or needed it.

It was Christmas time 1995. It was my third day away from home, and I had not heard from Paul. When I called home, there was no answer. I was becoming more concerned than I wanted to show. I wanted to rush home and see what was going on but I was committed to another two days of speaking.

Sleep did not come easily that night. I tried phoning home every half hour until well past midnight. No answer. Just the long drawn out silences between rings. I could not begin to imagine where Paul or the children could be. There was no reason for them to be away from home on a school night.

The next morning I felt like I had been beaten up. My eyes were puffy from crying, and I had a splitting headache. There would be a large group of women at the meeting and many of them would need my encouragement. I needed to give them my best but I felt my worst.

Just as we were leaving the house on the fourth morning, the phone rang. It was for me.

"Hi" his voice was quiet and sounded weak.

"Hi – where have you been? I have been worried sick!"

"I was in an accident, but I am okay. I am in the hospital."

"An accident? Where are the kids?" I wasn't sure if I was angry or scared or relieved.

"I'll tell you about it when you get home. I was with two other people and someone turned left in front of us at a main intersection and hit us."

"Are you sure you are okay?"

"I'll be fine. How is the speaking going?"

Suddenly I was terrified. My babies were too young to fend for themselves. "Where in the world are the kids?"

"Sandy picked them up a couple days ago and they are staying at her place."

I had so many questions but time was passing quickly, and we were going to be late for the meeting. I made light of it to my hostess but it was difficult to wrap my head around the whole scenario.

Why was Paul in the city when he was supposed to be at home with the kids? How serious were his injuries? The answers would have to wait but it was difficult to be patient.

When I arrived home a couple days later, I wanted to report all the good things that had happened. So many women had been encouraged and shared their problems with me. It was uplifting to be a source of strength for them. But, I was more concerned about what had happened to Paul.

Paul began to explain what happened. "I decided to run into the city for the day and bumped into some friends. We had lunch together. I was entering the intersection at 41st and Cambie. On my left was a big truck that shielded me from the view of the guy turning left in front of me. He ran right into us."

"What did the doctors say? Is anything seriously wrong?"

"My head was whipped back at rocket speed and it felt like my arm was ripped from its socket. I blacked out for a few seconds and when I opened my eyes there was a paramedic leaning over me telling me not to move. I found out later he was the guy who hit me. My shoulder is pretty beat up and I hit my head quite hard. You can't believe the headaches, but I am sure they will go away soon."

I was relieved that he was fine and that the kids were safe and so thankful that Sandy was able to look after Jason and Rochelle. They had come home from school and dad wasn't home. When it started to get late, they called Sandy and she picked them up. She had no way to contact me and no idea where Paul was. She kept them calm and assured them everything was all right.

After the accident, Paul continued seeing doctors regularly. They sent him to one specialist after another, 17 in all. None of them could completely understand why he was not improving. The next two years were exceptionally difficult.

Paul tried working shortly after the accident, but it wasn't long before he just could not do it anymore. He was taking so many pain killers but they were barely easing the pain.

Nine months passed and we were told that he had suffered a stroke after the accident. This was a result of the initial impact when his seat belt cut into his neck and sent a blood clot to his brain where it solidified deep in the basal ganglia. Eventually, this caused a movement disorder from nerve damage called dystonia.

Paul was prescribed narcotics to handle the pain and heavy doses of sleeping pills to get through the night. The drugs did not seem to help. He was diagnosed with Chronic Central Pain Syndrome and it was explained to us that because the thalamus, the sensory part of the brain, was damaged from the stroke, Paul's brain was sending signals that he was in constant pain. It was actually a phantom pain which the drugs could not possibly alleviate.

One of the medications was a combination of morphine and cocaine which caused unpredictable rage, violent temper and mood swings. To help calm himself he started smoking. I felt like giving up. I hated cigarette smoke and was severely allergic to it. I was worried this was a sign of something worse, something that would take control. It almost broke me.

Paul spent most of his days researching his case against the insurance company. Fortunately, they gave us living expenses until the case was settled. He talked to his lawyer several times a week and was keeping a log of his symptoms as they changed often. He was depressed and lost his self-worth. Staying involved with his insurance claim was like a job for him.

One of his doctors was a neuropsychiatrist at the University Hospital. He had a phenomenal bedside manner and regularly called Paul for updates to his progress. On one of these occasions, he asked to speak to me.

"How are you doing, Carol, really doing?" I held back the tears as I told him how difficult it was.

"There are days when Paul is so weak and disorientated he cannot feed himself. He suffers from severe hot flashes and strips off all his clothes to try to cool down. One day, when it was freezing outside, he stripped down and ran in the ocean. Then there are days when he is like a maniac. I can't handle the rage anymore. He is malicious to me. I know he has no control over this but that does not make it any easier. Some days he talks about killing himself and has threatened me as well."

"I understand, Carol. I want you to know that I have counselled many patients with brain injury and in 98% of the cases, the marriages do not last. The spouse cannot cope. My hat is off to you. I know you are strong and that is such a help to Paul. He has actually cried in my office telling me how he knows he has hurt you. We are going to figure this out and get his medications worked out so that both of you can have some quality of life. I am going to schedule a hospital stay for him to see if we can regulate his medications." I thanked him but didn't hold much optimism. It was a day-to-day struggle.

One of the new medications the doctors offered Paul gave him adrenaline rushes where he could not sit down for up to 16 hours at a time. He would run around the house and down the street. He lost 50 pounds in three weeks. I could see the sadness and terror in our children's eyes, and I did not know what else to do but to keep praying. My only hope was to trust God. There was nowhere else to turn.

The only way he could sleep was a heavy dose of medication. I had to be careful when he took the sleeping pills as it was extremely dangerous if taken too close to his other medications. Without my knowledge, one day he took an extra pain pill to try and get some relief.

It was a Friday night and Rochelle had a friend staying over. We were watching a movie and eating popcorn when the girls started to giggle. Paul was stuffing as much popcorn into his mouth as he could and it was coming out as fast as he pushed it in. He began to hallucinate.

"Why don't you girls buy those boots as long as we are in the mall?" They continued to snicker as he said things that were total nonsense. I had no idea he was on an extra pill.

"I'm going upstairs to put on my roller skates." He went upstairs to the bedroom and put on a suit and tie over his T-shirt. Then he put on his shoes, no socks, took some floor wax to tame his hair and announced he was going out dancing. It was August and there was an outdoor Country Music Festival about two miles from us. The music was loud enough to hear from inside our home. I chuckled to myself thinking how funny it would be to attend the festival in his condition. He moved like a drunken toddler. Even though I was concerned with this unusual behavior, it was good to have this laugh and it seemed a lot easier to cope with than anger.

I helped him get ready for bed and he took his sleeping pill. The pills were so strong that they always knocked him out in a matter of a few minutes. He would sleep deeply for several hours and there was no waking him.

He fell asleep and I realized something was wrong. He was not breathing. I called 911 and they put me in touch with Poison Control Center in Vancouver. The doctors at our local hospital were on strike and there was no one in emergency to attend patients. Poison Control was very sorry but it was a holiday weekend and staff was limited as well. They tutored me in how to arouse him and told me that I must make sure he was fully awake and did not stop breathing again. When I told them the medication he was on, they said he had obviously overdosed, and I could only hope for the best. I never felt so powerless.

I stayed up all night and held his wrist so I could feel his heartbeat. When he slowly woke in the morning, I was fully relieved believing the worst was over and this was a new day. Usually, it would take most of the day for him to be fully alert from the sleeping pills. He usually dozed all morning and then spent the rest of the day on the sofa. He was shaking most of the time and had difficulty holding a fork or a cup of coffee.

The stroke had caused damage to his left side and his leg and foot would often seize and go into spasm. He would fall down. He would hyperventilate, and I would get a paper bag to put over his head to calm him down. I was afraid to leave him alone – ever.

Friends were beginning to distance themselves at a rapid rate. I began to look forward to Paul going into the hospital in hopes of getting some rest and maybe a chance to have coffee with someone.

Jason was 17 years old and our chaotic lifestyle was taking a major toll on him. Sometimes he would cry and tell me how unfair this was. He loved his dad so much and it was extremely difficult for him to watch him suffer. None of us understood it and I certainly didn't have any solutions.

Rochelle was struggling a lot but had such powerful faith it was an encouragement to me. She kept telling me how strong I was and that she respected me for staying resilient. Watching my children gave me hope. Love would get us through this.

Paul was booked into University Hospital for three weeks. Because his doctor was a neuropsychiatrist, he was booked into the Psyche Ward. Taking a look around, I didn't want to leave him there. The smell was stale from either urine or bleach. His room had a cot, a bedside table and a small chest of drawers. It was neat and orderly but far from clean. I swallowed hard.

"Are you sure you will be okay here? Do you want me to see if we can get you into a different ward or room?"

"I'll be fine. I just want to find out what is going on so I can get on with some sort of life."

Walking through the hall felt like walking through the insane asylum I once saw in a movie. It was frightening, yet I knew all the patients were heavily sedated and posed no threats. I had a flash of Paul blindly walking down the halls, drooling and talking to himself. It made me shudder.

The idea of the hospital stay was to go through monitored withdrawal from the heavy medication and yet control the pain.

Paul was allowed one phone call a day and when he called me I could hear the agitation in his voice.

"I have NO idea why they put me in here. This is for loonies and if I stay here long enough I will be one of them."

I admitted he was right but encouraged him to be patient. If they could regulate the pain, we could maybe get back to a normal life and he could work again.

He continued, "The only way to pass any time is to watch TV and there is only one small TV in the lounge area and ONE remote. Just about everybody in the lounge is asleep except this one guy who believes he is in charge. He will not let me have the remote and he just flicks through the channels as fast as he can. It is driving me insane, LITERALY!"

I tried not to laugh out loud as I was imaging what this looked like. Frankly, I was enjoying a few days of peace at home. It was also great to have the TV remote to myself without Paul flicking through the channels. I didn't tell him that.

Unfortunately, after four days, the hospital nurses went on strike, again! Any patient who was not in a life and death situation had to be released. So, those four days were a complete waste of time. Nothing was accomplished and the experiment was done in vain.

I couldn't get him home fast enough as he reeked of, well, I am not sure what he reeked of but it was putrid. We were back to square one. We continued to trust God that he would give the doctors wisdom and find a solution. We believed for total restoration but the trial of our faith was just that – a trial.

As the lawyers continued to build our case against the insurance company, it became more and more exasperating. The insurance adjustors insisted on more tests and therapies, ranging from hypnosis to CAT Scans, MRI's and different medications. It was a full-time job for me to chauffeur him to doctors' and lawyers' offices. We were running out of funds and the insurance adjustor said there would be no more cash advances.

Our lawyers warned us that we were being watched. They said we were under video surveillance as the insurance company wanted to catch Paul doing something he said he would not be able to do. There was no reason for us to be careful about anything because Paul was not able to do much and that was a fact.

One morning Paul left Sheba, our elderly dog, outside and she did not come back. He got worried about her and went looking for her. He found her lying on the ground under some brush in the front yard. With all the strength he could muster, he gently picked her up and carried her into the house. She just lay on the kitchen floor. Every once in a while she would have what appeared to be a slight seizure. She was failing quickly.

Sheba was part of our family for 13 years. She loved each of us and showed her affection regularly. There were many nights she licked my tears. She would cuddle up to Jason or Rochelle and they knew she understood their pain. She was a treasure.

It was mid-afternoon and school would be out soon. I was not able to reach Jason but knew that Rochelle was in class and I had to get her home quickly. I sped down the streets, ran into her classroom and blurted something about an emergency to her teacher.

"Honey, we have an emergency – get in the car quickly. I think Sheba is dying. If you want to see her, we have to run now!"

Rochelle began to cry and it was difficult to watch. I was feeling her hurt and dealing with my own. She ran into the house and saw Sheba lying on the floor, unable to move. She gently picked up her friend's head and laid it on her lap. She proceeded to softly rub her and scratch behind her ears. With all the strength Sheba could muster, she lifted her head and let out a loud yelp. We all sobbed. Our beloved friend was gone. We didn't know what happened to her but guessed it was a heart attack. She was so much a part of our lives. She was special and could never be replaced.

Shortly after, Jason arrived home and I had to tell him what happened. Wiping the tears from his eyes, he got a blanket and covered her. Taking charge of the situation, he said he wanted to bury her on the mountain top where she loved to roam on their hikes together.

He didn't want his dad's help. We understood and allowed him to wrap her and place her in the trunk of the car. Paul drove with him up the mountain to the spot, overlooking the whole town, where Sheba loved to play.

Jason told me later about how he dug the hole and Paul helped lift her out of the trunk. Just as they were lifting her out, Jason spotted a flash of something shiny in the distance. He looked carefully and noticed someone taking videos of them. They were slightly concerned that someone might think they were lifting a human body out of the trunk as Sheba was a large dog wrapped in a blanket, making her appear larger still.

Later, we realized it was probably the insurance investigator spying on them. We were only somewhat apprehensive while at the same time felt like our privacy had been violated.

Our patience was wearing thin but finally we were given a date for Discovery and Mediation. Both of these conferences were full days of interrogation. Paul was questioned to the point of exhaustion. I had to remain in the lobby and wait out the many hours wondering what was going on behind closed doors. I was very upset that I was not allowed to be with him but there was nothing I could do about it. At the end of the day, it was determined we would be going to court and the date was set for the following year, 2002.

Our family had suffered through seven long years of waiting but soon it would be over. The settlement would take a lot of pressure off of us, especially Paul who was struggling daily with not being able to support his family. The kids and I had to constantly walk on egg shells – not knowing what might trigger Paul's anger. Our lawyers were asking for over 1.5 million dollars to cover pain and suffering and living expenses for the rest of Paul's life.

Over the past couple years, we had a feeling our lawyers were working against us instead of for us. It was very difficult to determine or understand; but at one point, Paul tried to fire them and they convinced him into reconsidering. We couldn't put our fingers on it but knew something wasn't right. They became evasive and disinterested in our case. Originally, they consistently encouraged Paul and told him that they were going for the jugular and he would be set for life.

At the last meeting we had with the lawyers, they explained

the court procedure and we should be confidant they would walk him through all possible scenarios. They scheduled a mock trial at their offices for the following week and asked if Paul would be able to drive to Vancouver by himself because it was not necessary that I be there.

"It will be a boring, long day and there is really no reason for you to waste your time, Carol." I felt relieved at the thought of a day to myself and confidant this would all be over very soon. Paul was getting strong enough to drive himself so I agreed to stay home. I had no idea what our lawyers had planned and no indication that something was amiss.

Paul arrived at the law office early that Friday morning. The lawyers told him that they were actually going to the court house instead. Paul was very confused and his pain level was escalating. The insurance company's lawyers, our lawyers, and Paul were waiting in the lobby and he was still completely unaware what was transpiring. The two sets of lawyers were conversing in hushed tones and Paul was becoming agitated and very suspicious that something was seriously wrong.

Paul's case number was called and they filed into the court room. He was still under the impression that this was going to be a mock trial as we were told. He had no reason to think otherwise.

Paul was called before the judge.

"Mr. Graham, I have taken some time to review your case and although you have 17 specialists who concur that there is evidence your brain injury was caused by your accident in 1995, there is no solid evidence to corroborate that. Therefore, I see no reason for this case to go to trial and I suggest, Mr. Graham, you go into the conference room and settle this case today."

By early afternoon I was getting concerned. Why didn't I go with him? I shouldn't have let him drive by himself. Why doesn't he call? This is taking far too long. I began to pace and tried to keep my focus positive. However, something didn't feel right.

Paul had taken several more pain killers and was having difficulty focusing. He believed the court-ordered conference would be in his favor and a settlement would finally be reached. Sitting in a room full of lawyers he felt like an island. The pain was intense and he was wavering between agitation and complacency. Finally, an agreement was reached and Paul left to call me.

"Hi honey. It's over."

"That's good. I was starting to worry because I haven't heard from you at all. So you are ready for court next week?"

"Don't you understand? I said it was over."

"What's over? What are you talking about?"

I could hear him take a deep breath. "I settled the case today."

"YOU WHAT?"

"Don't worry, everything is great. I will explain it all when I get home. I will be getting a check next week. It's finally OVER!"

I still could not believe my ears. How could it be over when so much planning had gone into the trial? Why didn't we have a chance to plead our case after so many years of preparation?

"How much did you settle for?"

"$250,000. Of course, the lawyers will take their fees but we will be fine. I am getting better every day and will be able to invest or do whatever I have to do without worrying about the case or the insurance company spying on us."

When he got home he told me all about the conference. By now, he was thinking more clearly and was gravely troubled that something had been terribly wrong. The more he thought about it the more he began to doubt that his lawyers were working on his behalf.

After legal fees, cash advances for five years, all the specialist's visits, expenses and taxes were taken out of our settlement; we walked away with a check for less than $50,000. I stared at it. I kept thinking they must be missing a zero. How could we live on this for the rest of our lives? What were we going to do? I was angry, sad, confused, frustrated and yet relieved it was over.

Paul continued to study all the documents he received at the settlement conference and the figures would not compute. He finally realized that the lawyers had taken an extra five percent than we had originally agreed. We registered a claim against the firm and went before a judge suing the main lawyer in our case.

After hearing our evidence, the judge looked at our lawyer, and shook his finger at him as if to scold a young child.

"You were a fool to try to pull something like this over your client. You should be ashamed of yourself and you should know better."

He raised the gavel and found in our favor and told the lawyer he had two days to return the $12,000 he had stolen from us.

Years later, when Paul spoke to another lawyer about the case, he was convinced that Paul was taken advantage of. He was confidentially told that our lawyers had a bad reputation, and it was very possible that monies and/or favors had been exchanged between the two sides to make our case go away quickly. It would be very difficult to reopen the case but this lawyer was pushing us to do just that. We absolutely could not open that can of worms. As much as we knew we had been treated unfairly and unjustly, we did not have the energy.

We wanted to live our lives and put this behind us. Paul had established a relationship over the years with Rob, who lived in the valley, East of Vancouver. Rob had purchased 40 acres of land that he wanted to log off. He asked Paul to partner with him. The plan was to sell the logs and then sell the property.

As difficult as it was for Paul, in order for us to have any kind of income, he would have to work the property by preparing the logs for the logging company. It was incredibly strenuous labor. When the trees were cut down, he removed all the branches and cleared all the debris so the logging company could pick up the timber. He certainly was getting in physical shape but his pain level only escalated. He pushed himself to the max - worked three weeks straight and then came home for a few days. We estimated it would take about three years to clear the land and then we would decide if we would build on it, or sell it as is. Property values were going up in the area.

In the meantime, I was maintaining a small, internet, eBay business selling gemstones we had acquired over the past several years. Paul had invested in gemstones whenever possible to build a nest egg for our future. I enjoyed contributing my time and managed to stay quite busy.

After a year of working the land, we decided to buy the next parcel of an additional 40 acres. As difficult as it was for Paul to do this kind of labor, he felt great seeing what he was accomplishing. There was a large house on the property and our partner suggested a friend of his rent it and act as caretaker.

The next couple years were busy and productive. But the labor had taken its toll on Paul. He had lost far too much weight and was looking worn out all the time. He had fallen off a log and cracked a couple ribs adding more pain than he was already experiencing. He seemed to be depressed, and it was always very difficult for him to go back to work after being home a few days. He could not continue doing that kind of physical activity any longer. Fortunately, our eBay business had grown and we were able to have a steady income from that. So we decided to concentrate on that and work together from home.

Paul had always dreamed of opening a youth center, and we decided to purchase a building downtown Sechelt to fulfil that dream. Everything was falling into place, and we were excited to make a contribution to our community's youth. We did not want it to be a typical drop-in center but wanted more of a club atmosphere. We purchased enough sound equipment to construct a complete recording studio. The building was big enough to have the sound studio on one end and a recreation room with big screen televisions for teens to play video games and interact in a safe environment. We built a snack and drink bar and there was an excitement materializing in the community for opening day.

We did, however, face some objections from the more mature population. They were afraid the center would become a hangout for kids to buy and sell drugs. A campaign to abort the project began before we had a chance to prove otherwise. Consequently, we were not able to get the necessary permits and had to stop production. Paul's dream was shattered. It felt like a hard slap in the face.

We had exhausted our financial resources to get this off the ground and our only option at this point was to sell the building – fast. We had four offers the first week, and we ended up selling way too low, too soon.

At least we knew that we had given it our best and maybe we could try again elsewhere. We located a warehouse to store all the sound equipment and assumed we would only need it for a short term before we found a better storage facility.

We did not live on the premises so the insurance company only allowed $50,000 insurance on the contents of the building. Paul didn't want to bother with insurance, but I felt that some insurance was better than none at all.

It was November. The skies were dark and winter was settling in with lots of rain. We were living in a rural area near the ocean. Our rental house had a large deck that had never been treated properly against the elements. In the early mornings when I let the dogs outside, I needed to be very careful because the deck was particularly slippery.

I rose early one morning as we planned to go to the city to buy a much needed car. I let the dogs out and was standing on the edge of the deck watching them in the yard. They were approaching the house as I turned to go back inside. My feet slipped out from under me and I slid right off the edge of the deck onto the stairs. The center of my back hit the edge of the second wooden step.

The loud crack I heard sent terror up my spine and the wind was knocked out of me. I honestly thought I was going to die. Thoughts were racing through my head wondering if Paul would rescue me in time. My dogs knew something was wrong and were trying to lick my face as I lay there unable to move.

I called out "Babe!" No matter how loud I cried it was barely a whisper.

I would work up another breath and yell "BABE!" Nothing came out.

I couldn't move. I could barely breathe. It was far too early in the morning for Paul to be up and I did not know what to do. My legs were twisted behind me and the pain was almost unbearable. An eternity passed until Paul finally came out onto the deck.

"Why are you laying there?" I am sure he was not awake enough to realize I was in serious trouble. By this time, I was able to speak in a whisper and as Paul helped me up, I hoped I was all right.

Very cautiously, he helped me into the house and I sat down. The pain was terrible. I assumed I cracked a rib. We were supposed to go to the city that day to buy a car and were planning to spend the night with friends.

I did not want to put a damper on our plans so I took a couple of Paul's strong pain killers and prepared to go. If I had a cracked rib, I knew the doctor would only tell me to rest and give me pain killers anyway.

When we got to the city, my breathing was labored and painful and I worried that my lung was punctured. Paul could see my distress and took me into emergency.

The nurse said, "Get up onto the bed and we'll have the doctor examine you. If he thinks it is necessary, we will get an X-ray."

I could not believe how nonchalant she was. She did not offer to help me up onto the examining table. I was expected to do this alone. The emergency doctor asked me some questions and only did a minimal examination.

"It does not appear that anything is broken and your X ray did not show any fractures so go home and take it easy. You should be as good as new in a few days." I wanted to believe him, but I was in severe pain, worse than any car accident.

We did buy the car and each time Paul shifted gears I thought I was going to stop breathing. The pain was escalating and any sharp movement aggravated it. I took more pain killers so we could have dinner with our friends and try to enjoy the evening.

I was glad when the evening was over and we could go to bed. Sleep was difficult and around 3:00 A. M. I woke up with a start. Something was frightfully wrong and I felt the urgency to pray. I prayed for protection for myself and my family and that God would intervene in whatever area He needed to.

I drifted back to sleep until their house phone rang at 5:00 A. M. It rang and rang and then stopped. I felt very uneasy and did not understand why our friends had not answered the call. About 15 minutes later, it rang again. After three rings, I picked it up. It was my daughter.

"Mom, you need to call Jason right away. He has been trying to reach you."

"Why, what's wrong?" My voice was shaking.

"I don't know exactly but I think the warehouse is burning down."

"WHAT? What are you talking about?" What she said would not register.

"Just call him, Mom and hurry!"

My hands were shaking as I handed the phone to Paul. "Call Jason – the shop is burning down."

Secretly I was hoping it was either a bad dream or a great exaggeration by my daughter. It was neither. It was true.

We rushed to get on the first ferry back home and went immediately to the property. Nothing prepared us for what we saw. Jason lived on the property adjacent to the shop, and he was visibly shaken when we arrived.

"You just can't believe it. I never saw anything like it. We didn't have a hope to stop it. I'm so sorry." Paul calmed him and asked him what happened.

"The dog was barking like crazy, and I kept telling her to shut up but she wouldn't listen. I finally went over to the door and saw flames coming from the warehouse. I grabbed the handle to the sliding glass door and it was so hot I burned my hand. I knew I needed to move my truck 'cuz it was so close to the shop, so I ran out there. You wouldn't believe the heat. I was running towards the truck and I watched the gas tank fall off. Gas was spilling all over the place and then hit the flames. It was surrounding me and I had to run back. Just as I did that, the truck blew up."

"Thank God you weren't hurt!" I was holding back the tears.

We had recently purchased a large compressor for Jason to use when he worked on vehicles. He had just assembled it and started to use it the day before. We found out later that was a phenomenal blessing in disguise. When the compressor blew, it was an amazing explosion but the fire chief said if the hoses had not been attached there would have been 6,000 pounds of pressure, which could have sent metal and debris to the surrounding homes and the people sleeping inside.

It only took about 11 minutes for the building to burn to the ground.

We had stored all the sound equipment in there along with a lot of other things including the boat Jason had inherited from his grandfather, his motorbike and three classic cars we were restoring.

We felt a mixture of hopelessness and despair. Once again we were emotionally spent and wondering why.

I was so grateful we had put insurance on it after all. Even though the insurance was only $50,000 and the financial loss was $350,000, the emotional loss was greater. So many memories and hopes were destroyed. Rochelle's boyfriend, Thomas, had also used the space to store personal items. One was a box of pictures and momentoes of his mom, who died when he was a little boy. I felt sick to my stomach about the whole ordeal

The insurance company interrogated us and intimated that we set the fire to collect the insurance. That was asinine if they considered the amount of the loss against the amount of the insurance. In time, it was determined that the fire was deliberately set to satisfy the warped mind of a drugged local arsonist. Within six months, we were granted the settlement but it did little to appease the situation.

I continued to be in constant pain from my back and my physical activity was very limited. I could only stand for a few minutes at a time. Housework and cooking were extremely difficult.

I tried various methods for relief including massage, chiropractic treatments, heat therapy, and painkillers. Nothing seemed to help. After two years, my doctor suggested another X-ray. But this time he wanted a picture of my spine, not my ribs. When the results came back, he called me into his office.

"Read this!" He tossed the report in my direction with a smile on his face.

When I read it, a tear ran down my cheek. I was right. Something was gravely wrong. The tear was mixed emotion. I was scared when I read it and relieved that my pain was not imagined. My back had been broken; my spine fractured.

"Now, get yourself a lawyer, Carol. You will need it. This is not going away. You need legal advice on how to get compensated for this tragedy."

Fortunately, I hired excellent lawyers and made an out-of-court settlement for my fractured back five years later.

Finally, life had some solidity. We thanked God for his many blessings for us and our children. Our eBay business continued to grow and we were getting an income from the property up north.

Our children were now grown and started their own lives outside the home. Jason married his sweetheart of three years, Rachael. They had a beautiful wedding on the beach of a local lake, and we were delighted to see him so happy. Rochelle had also made a commitment to Thomas. She attended the Gemological Institute of America in California graduating with honors as a gemologist.

Paul was no longer physically able to work the property up north, and we were having a difficult time keeping up with our share of the mortgage payments. We were trying to make a decision about what to do when we got a shocking phone call from our partner, Rob.

"You are not going to believe this! That jerk who was renting the house had a grow op in there."

"What do you mean?" It wasn't registering with Paul.

"I mean that the cops showed up and didn't even bother opening the gate – they just drove through it and ripped the fence down."

"What in the world triggered them to do that?" It just wasn't making any sense. We hadn't been to the property for a long time but had no idea there was a problem.

"The stupid guy ran up a huge bill with the hydro company and they called the cops to investigate."

Paul was extremely upset; but we knew that it had nothing to do with us and assumed the guy would be arrested and we would just rent it to someone else. When I got the hydro bill a week later I almost collapsed. It was for $29,000.

After many conversations and arguments with the hydro company they told us the bottom line was that we, as landlords, were responsible to know what was going on with our property.

When the case against the tenant went to court, he pled guilty and we thought that would relieve us from the debt. We were wrong. The hydro company said the tenant had no means of paying the bill and it would be our responsibility.

With the high mortgage payment and now this impending debt, Rob suggested we sell our portion of the property to him and he would make our share of the mortgage payments as well as his. He didn't have the funds to buy us out so suggested we sign over our portion of the 80 acres to him for one dollar; and when he sold it, we would get our investment back plus half the profit. We did just that and that was the last time we saw or heard from him. After a couple months, I called the lady at the hydro office who we had been dealing with. I left a long detailed message on her voice mail, that we did not have the means to pay that bill and did not believe we should be responsible for it. I was clear and matter of fact. It still concerned me for a few months but as time went on, I realized they had dropped the case and we never heard from them again.

Over the years I often had been asked if I ever got mad at God. I have never understood that question. What did God have to do with our bad decisions, our mistakes, and our failures? It was true that many things happened that were not our fault but were all part of life. We were vividly aware that no matter what happened to us, God was there to sustain us, to give us courage and strength and to help us see the blessing that came with every trial. The biggest question I had was, "How do people go through the trials of life without God to lean on?"

There were a lot of times I felt like giving up. But I always felt encouraged that God did not want that for me. There was a lot I did not understand and probably never would. But I also knew that He cared for me, loved me and would never leave me.

The next decade proved just that. We began to see what had happened in our lives was to prepare us for what was ahead. The difficult lessons we learned were to help us with making wise decisions for the future.

We were able to open three jewelry stores and my Shaklee business began to flourish. Our son and daughter-in-law gave us two beautiful grandsons and our daughter and her husband gave us a grandson as well. Nothing, absolutely nothing, could have given us more joy.

Paul made about an 80% recovery, and we are continuing to trust for 100%. Life still has its challenges but experience is a great teacher. We continue to stay focused, driven, and motivated. We offer encouragement and strength to so many people who are distraught and defeated. Because of everything we went through; we have empathy and offer hope.

We recently celebrated our fortieth wedding anniversary with friends and family. Reflecting on the past, we realize how quickly it has gone and how strong and focused we have become. We have grown to love each other deeper and are partners in every respect. Paul's mother passed away at the age of 95. We were so blessed to have had her in our lives for so many years and for her encouragement and prayers which were unending. I have continued to grow closer to my sister and brother over these past couple decades and am so thankful for their support.

I continue to share at CWC, and we are involved in our church. We have wonderful friends around us who have been a source of support and love. Our children and grandchildren bring us the joy that I had prayed and hoped for in the early years.

Sometimes it seems like I am a magnet for people who have diverse and serious troubles. I listen, encourage and often relate. Had I not had the experiences of the past, I would not be able to empathize now. For that I am thankful.

Contact the Author at:
batteredhope@gmail.com